THE ARGOT MERCHANT DISASTER

ALSO BY GEORGE STARBUCK

Bone Thoughts
White Paper
Elegy in a Country Church Yard
Desperate Measures
Talkin' B.A. Blues

George Starbuck

**THE
ARGOT MERCHANT
DISASTER**

**Poems
New and Selected**

An Atlantic Monthly Press Book
Little, Brown and Company
Boston / Toronto

FIRST EDITION

The poems in IV are from *Desperate Measures* by George Starbuck. Copyright © 1978 by George Starbuck. Reprinted by permission to David R. Godine, Publisher, Inc.

Library of Congress Cataloging in Publication Data

Starbuck, George, 1931–
  The argot merchant disaster.

  "An Atlantic Monthly Press book."
  I. Title.
PS3569.T3356A88 811'.54   82-7792
ISBN 0-316-81084-3   AACR2
ISBN 0-316-81081-9 (pbk.)

ATLANTIC—LITTLE, BROWN BOOKS
ARE PUBLISHED BY
LITTLE, BROWN AND COMPANY
IN ASSOCIATION WITH
THE ATLANTIC MONTHLY PRESS

BP

Designed by Janis Capone

Published simultaneously in Canada
by Little, Brown & Company (Canada) Limited

PRINTED IN THE UNITED STATES OF AMERICA

To George W. Beiswanger,
   critic and teacher,
   who has been a father to me.

CONTENTS

3. CRITICAL SHORTAGES
(poems from the 1960s, from the book White Paper)

4. WARPAINT
(poems from the 1970s, from the book Desperate Measures)

I.

Thin Ice

THIN ICE

POEMS FROM THE 1980s

COMMENCEMENT ADDRESS

You are the retribution we invoke.
You are the sudden daybreak we proclaim.
We flock to the unburdening: our shame
Is History: pale alibi: bad joke.

A mud of Nothing labored and awoke.
A spawn of cities crumbled into flame.
A galloping of paladins became
Nightmare and died screaming when it foaled you.

The nebulae come running to behold you.
If it were not so I would have told you.
Surely goodness and mercy are the name
The darkness and the starry legions spoke
When they cast down their banners to enfold you
In the sparse tangled buntings of the dawn.

3

MAGNIFICAT IN TRANSIT
FROM THE TOLEDO AIRPORT

The world has a glass center.
I saw the sign for it.

TOLEDO, GLASS CENTER OF THE WORLD

That's what surprised me.
I mean that it was Toledo.
I knew the center was glass.
That's why we've got this cleaning-and-polishing operation going.
There were bulldozers outside of Toledo, working away.

It's a beginning.
Move this junk, we'll be able to see in.
When the Chinamen at the other end gear up, we'll be able to see through.
It's like the completion of the first transcontinental railroad.

It's like what the Egyptians had in mind when they invented the pyramids.
It's like what God would have opted for if he had been an optician.
There it'll be.
This really tremendous lens.

Think of the excitement when they put the ceremonial white handkerchief
into the outstretched hand of the Final Polisher.
What if he suddenly thinks he's Sonja Henie?
What if he just gets awestruck and sits down?

Actually there'll be an airtight operating procedure.
Polish it off. Take measurements. Melt in.

You can do that, when it's glass.
Goes into what they call a "solid solution."
"Doping the mix," they call it. Vary the additive
and the whole ball of glass comes out in a wonderful color:
rose. ultramarine. turquoise. maroon.
It's enough to make you lose your marbles.

It *is* a marble.

4

I know all about marbles, I said, this is my bag!
Will it be a milkie? Will it be a purie? Will it be a swirl?
"Oh get more bulldozers, Ohio," I said to myself in a fit of eloquence.
"Toledo *is* the glass center of the world."

I felt like the *Boy's Life* monthly good luck stories.
"Cabin Boy with Columbus." "Young Hank Ford."

I always liked the one where the safari
saves me (I've just been orphaned by the Zulu)
and lets me tag along with them up country
into the wild unknown Witwatersrand.
You know the story: how the evil porter
filches the beads, and fills the bags with stones.

Toledo Toledo, I warbled,
even though this Red Yellow Cab Company taxicab is bearing me away
        from you at maximum achievable velocity,
even though my appointment is in Bowling Green,
I shall push in the press for deployment of Project Ploughshare.
I shall lobby. I shall make mailings. I shall crusade.
Instant redistribution of silage among the developed peoples!
Riverbanks full of afterburgers! Boom!
Is there a high-gain, high-risk, maximum-impact slot in there somewhere for
        a creative projects person with hands-on image-management experience
        and a desire to position himself on the forefront of America's growth
        industry for the 1990s?
Toledo, I have arrived!

I have arrived in Bowling Green.

Bowling Green State, the Athens of the Midwest.

Emptiness. Houses. Emptiness-houses. Shrublets.
Grass. What am I doing here? This trike.

Here, from his door, to my rescue, comes my host.
He is Ray DiPalma.
He is a poet.
He is from Pittsburgh, Steel Center of the World.

Oh damn. Wouldn't you know? He is. It's true.

5

He is from Pittsburgh Steel Center of the World
And *I* knew that. *I* used to have a steelie.
Too heavy, they said, that's cheating, you go home.

You ever look down deep into a steelie?
Really strange reflections.
Whole horizon.
You! bigger than everybody's houses.
Big-nose.
Steely little eyes.

You know what's wrong with American free enterprise?
It's two-bit people in two-bit little places
doin' a two-bit number on theirselves.

Myself I know the world has a glass center.
Myself I know it's Toledo, built on sand.
And soon now, in the place of the bulldozer,
soon now, under the battlements and banners,
rose, ultramarine, turquoise, maroon,
this scraggy ol', scruffy ol', vermin-infested slagpile,
this rubble-in-arms, gonna sing out loud an' clear,
like a great bell, like the choir of all the angles.
I'll get more dope on it as soon as I get home to Iowa City.

Iowa City — the Athens of the Midwest.
I have a friend there in the Pittsburgh Plate Glass Company.
Damned if it isn't true — Pittsburgh Plate Glass.

Not Pittsburgh Paint now, mind you. Pittsburgh Paint
sells glass put out by Owens Illinois.
At least that's what it does in Iowa.
Or did, when I last had a broken window.
To tell the truth, that was a while ago.
Recently I've been living in New Hampshire.

They make a claim there about maple syrup
but I say let's pretend they never said it.

I mean I'm all for backwoods boosterism
but when you start to ask folks to believe

this mighty item all wrapped up in blue,
this whopping gobbet of long-lasting goodness,
this great big hunk, this Earth, this greater Mars,
is something with a novelty interior —
a sort of oversized designer chocolate —
well that's beyond preposterous. That's dumb.

Sometimes when I consider how this world
is given to outright exaggeration,
I think I should've stood put in Columbus.

Columbus Ohio, the Athens of the Midwest.
Home of the mighty Buckeyes. I was born there
and moved away when I was four days old
and always like to tell it that way, acting
as if I'd sized the place up and skedaddled.

The Buckeyes are Ohio State of course.
Ohio State is not Ohio U.
Ohio U's a college, and a good one,
off in a little mill town name of Athens.
God knows what Athens is the Athens of.

Actual buckeyes — just in case you wondered —
Actual buckeyes are the kind of nut
you'd pick up off the sidewalks in October
and ram a toothpick into for a spindle
to hold a set of cut-out paper sails
and join Miss Dean's Columbus-Day flotilla
across the blue construction-paper ocean
to prove the world was chock-a-block with marvels
to *make* things out of, Right Beneath Your Feet.

I think she made me a Discoverer,
Miss Dean did. And Miss Whitman. And Miss Ide.
I got the real good news about creation.

Merciful Muchness, Principle of Redundance,
Light of the World converted at every turn,
the world *is* too much for us, wait and see!

SIGN

Virgin, sappy, gorgeous, the right-now
Flutters its huge prosthetics at us, flung
To the spotlights, frozen in motion, center-ice.

And the first rows, shaken with an afterslice
That's bowled them into their seats like a big wet ciao.
O daffy panoply O rare device

O flashing leg-iron at a whopping price
Whipping us into ecstasies and how,
The whole galumphing Garden swung and swung,

A rescue helicopter's bottom rung
Glinting and spinning off, a scud of fluff,
A slash of petals up against the bough,

A juggler's avalanche of silken stuff
Gushing in white-hot verticals among
Camels and axels and pyramids, oh wow,

Bewilderment is parachute enough.
We jolt. A sidewise stutterstep in chorus.
The other billboards flicker by before us.

Gone! with a budded petulance that stung.
So talented! So targeted! So young!
Such concentration on the bottom line!

We vanish down the IRT. A shine.
A glimmer. Something. Nothing. To think twice
Was to have lost the trick of paradise.

WORK SONG

tell me he don't go nowhere but he do.
Pigs an' the chickens could have him anymore.
Momma workin' her knuckles black an' blue
prettyin' me an' tellin' me the score
An' shoot. Twenty-eight years I don't say boo.

Things go, anymore, it's a dog's breakfast.
Things go, anymore, you'd as good go bust.
Ain't a brand-name contraption last the payments.
Moneyback politician you can trust.

Waaavin' the love-o'-God in people's faces
till you can't tell the grade school from a zoo.
Mrs. He-Loves-You Rogers come down Main Street
walkin' a rhinestone lapdog like some whore.
Shoot, chile. you go *lis'nin'* to me for?

Ain't nothin' but the flappin' noise us old folks
makes when the wind starts risin' in the yard.
Honey, if all that craziness an' romance
sat down on a person's heart so hard,

you think old Mrs. Hawes'd be out rakin'?
her with the one in Stateville, an' the one —
look at her out there, crazy in the sun —
you think she'd whoop herself into conniptions
chasin' Leota's twins right through the chard
an' whappin' with her cowboy bonnet after
a good two hundred pounds of St. Bernard?

Honey, come on now, pitch in, get 'em jarred.
It'll drive-time, an' Ba be home for supper,
an' Cronkite comin' on, an' be nothin' done

INCIDENT OF
THE BLIZZARD OF '81

Note: The "vanishing hitchhiker" is well at-
tested. Three incidents made the national news-
wires in 1980, and in the fall of 1981 a book
appeared, devoted to him and his reappear-
ances. Always, the hiker talks earnestly of reli-
gion. Always, at highway speed, the car door
opens, it must have opened, and the hiker is
gone.

I left Fat City, toolin' my Coupe de Gras.
I'm givin' them high-hatters the ha ha
Like J. Paul Getty if Getty had been the Shah.

Man with the map of neon in his eyeballs.
Wigwaggin' with a backpack full of Bibles
Next to the scorched blue chassis of a Ford.

Levels a sixpack at me. Swings aboard
And ballyhoos the good news of the Lord
From Cedar Rapids halfway to Grand Island.

Singin' his checkered pastureland is my land.
Settin' the Millers cans up single file and
Mowin' em down like Midianites. Nebraska

Vanished without a trace. No road, no landscape,
Just Kellogg's famous featherweight white breakfast
Shot from the snub-nose silos of the plains.

Seventy per and a prayer in place of chains,
Opens the door and gets out. Shit for brains.
Stunt like that he could pass for Lyndon Baines.

Before he left he spouted some damn doggerel
And handed me six tickets to the Inaugural.
Balls and all. That's how I met Carl Sagan

And got to shake the hand of Nancy Reagan
And heard that stuff about Menachim Begin
I told you back there west of Wichita?

HAIKU

Iowa crickets!
   I thought the VW
bearing was going.

ON GOZZOLI'S PAINTED
ROOM IN THE MEDICI PALACE

Lorenzo da Credi
Honored the Lord, St. Joseph, and Our Lady,
But not so hotsy-totsily
As did Benozzo Gozzoli.

What a parade. The sun
Bejewels everyone.
A barebones countryside
Stiffens to take magnificence in stride.

No wonder yokels gawk
And pieces of livestock
Go gallivanting gauchely while their lazy
Husbandmen (bunch of no-count Abruzzesi)

Loaf in a far-off byre
Where there might be a fire
(It's hard to make the glow out at this distance)
And mummers dance assistance

To someone in disguise.
He seems to be preparing a surprise
Tableau-vivant with Potentates and Peasants
And far-fetched birthday presents.

Never was sweeter, swifter, swanker, sportier
Caravan of the noble genus courtier
Visited on the sticks in one fell swoop.
It's every bit as special as the troop

Of lallygagging five-year-olds intuit.
How does Benozzo do it?
The whole old Christmas story,
The stagecraft, the accoutrements of glory

Huddled into a space about the size
Of that abstracted foreground horseman's eyes.

The one who watches us.
Alert, not curious.

Reserved, not bored.
This is the fit companion for a Lord.
A Lord himself, if destined.
None of your bullyragging, lead-intestined

Ravagers of the Apennines, but boss.
The man a man of judgment does not cross,
Ever.
Do not expect Benozzo to play clever.

His game is not distortion.
There is no disproportion
In anything he chooses, tells, or shows.
The facts are not Benozzo's to dispose.

A landscape has been blest.
The primacy of gentleness expressed.
And to a lady's credit she
Has been called on by a Medici.

CANON FANIN'S APOLOGY

"It is the right of the faithful not to be troubled
by theories and hypotheses that they are not
expert in judging . . ."
— John Paul II, Washington, Oct. '79

John Paul, you are a lovely man, a lovely man.
And I'm heartily sorry, heartily sorry I am
to see you be troubled now, to see you be seriously troubled
by all this theory-and-hypothesis, theory-and-hypothesis if I do say.

You have the right of it, Father, you have the right.
I cannot think what mischief it was that possessed us.
And sometimes it seems no end to the number of teachings.
And teachers beyond all reason it can sometimes seem.

And what can be quicker to break your heart and quicker
to pull down pride in a man than to see these faithful
lost in the terrible toils and the implications.

They worry a worry to death and they will not let go.

Woe be to the worrier of them then, the pernicious teacher.
Child against father he sets them, father against child.

THE SPELL
AGAINST SPELLING

(a poem to be inscribed in dark places and
never to be spoken aloud)

My favorite student lately is the one who wrote about feeling clumbsy.
I mean if he wanted to say how it feels to be all thumbs he
Certainly picked the write language to right in in the first place.
I mean better to clutter a word up like the old Hearst place
Than to just walk off the job and not give a dam.

Another student gave me a diagragm.
"The Diagragm of the Plot in Henry the VIIIth."

Those, though, were instances of the sublime.
The wonder is in the wonders they can come up with every time.

Why do they all say heighth, but never weighth?
If chrystal can look like English to them, how come chryptic can't?
I guess cwm, chthonic, qanat, or quattrocento
Always gets looked up. But never momento.
Momento they know. Like wierd. Like differant.
It is a part of their deep deep-structure vocabulary:
Their stone axe, their dark bent-offering to the gods:
Their protoCro-Magnon pre-pre-sapient survival-against-cultural-odds.

You won't get *me* deputized in some Spelling Constabulary.
I'd sooner abandon the bag-toke-whiff system and go decimal.
I'm on their side. I better be, after my brush with "infinitessimal."

There it was, right where I put it, in my brand-new book.
And my friend Peter Davison read it, and he gave me this look,
And he held the look for a little while and said, "George . . ."

I needed my students at that moment. I, their Scourge.
I needed them. Needed their sympathy. Needed their care.
"Their their," I needed to hear them say, "their their."

You see, there are *Spellers* in this world, I mean mean ones too.
They shadow us around like a posse of Joe Btfsplks

15

Waiting for us to sit down at our study-desks and go shrdlu
So they can pop in at the windows saying "tsk tsk."

I know they're there. I know where the beggars are,
With their flash cards looking like prescriptions for the catarrh
And their mnemnmonics, blast 'em. They go too farrh.
I do not stoop to impugn, indict, or condemn;
But I know how to get back at the likes of thegm.

For a long time, I keep mumb.
I let 'em wait, while a preternatural calmn
Rises to me from the depths of my upwardly opened palmb.
Then I raise my eyes like some wizened-and-wisened gnolmbn,
Stranger to scissors, stranger to razor and coslmbn,
And I fix those birds with my gaze till my gaze strikes hoslgmbn,
And I say one word, and the word that I say is "Oslgmbnh."

"Om?" they inquire. "No, not exactly. *Oslgmbnh.*
Watch me carefully while I pronounce it because you've got only two more
    guesses
And you only get one more hint: there's an odd number of esses,
And you only get ten more seconds no nine more seconds no eight
And a right answer doesn't count if it comes in late
And a wrong answer bumps you out of the losers' bracket
And disqualifies you for the National Spellathon Contestant jacket
And that's all the time extension you're going to gebt
So go pick up your consolation prizes from the usherebt
And don't be surprised if it's the bowdlerized regularized paperback
    abridgment of Pepys
Because around here, gentlemen, we play for kepys."

Then I drive off in my chauffeured Cadillac Fleetwood Brougham
Like something out of the last days of Fellini's Rougham
And leave them smiting their brows and exclaiming to each other
    "Ougham!
O-U-G-H-A-M Ougham!" and tearing their hair.

Intricate are the compoundments of despair.

Well, brevity must be the soul of something-or-other.

Not, certainly, of spelling, in the good old mother
Tongue of Shakespeare, Raleigh, Marvell, and Vaughan.
But something. One finds out as one goes aughan.

CALYPSO

Do I make sense?
Well I sorry if I do.
I tries to be so what.
Be crummy if I knew
How many sides my but
Been breaded on. Eheu.
Tiens.
L'amour est mort.
Vive la différence.
If every so often the dif has a dauphin
Honi soit qui mal y pense.
Spangle the little beggar and let him strut.
Count on it, eh what?
Magical Mardi-Gras messiness sweeps through,
Giving the heave-ho to the how-to.
Start up de whole shebang from de scratch scratch?
Natch.

THE SIXTH FLEET
STILL OUT THERE
IN THE MEDITERRANEAN

ΟΑΣΙΣ ΜΠΑΡ. OASIS BAR. To be an
Omnibus of immensity with a tin-can retinue.
To be cerulean, not herculean.
To shine against the bright blue empyrean
Bright as a dancer's eyelid, bright as the riffraff at a zoo
Crowding the bars with tidbits to poke through.
What an Odyssean outcome. What a coup.

The light grows positively Sophoclean.
Towerings and dishevelments ensue.
A slash of *zacharoplasteion* neon
Scribbles a wet hello all over the forefront of the view
And the little boats go loco. How are you?

O Cyruses, O Nelsons, you can see an
Aeon of our imperium all hung up and hove-to.
Azure bespangled enormous immobile blue
Pig eyes parsing the vintages: ΓΚΡΑ ΚΡΟΥ.

GREETING

Beautiful day.
Beautiful day.
Beautiful day.
What a dumb dumb-dumb song the old man sings.
Turning the compost,
Changing a lightswitch,
Grouting things.

18

THE GREAT DAM
DISASTER A BALLAD

to Kathy

Have you heard of the great dam disaster
When the flood control project gave way?
They were searchin' for seven days after.
Then the search party called it a day.

Then the Sheriff drove up in his flivver.
Then the widow collapsed and despaired,
While a couple of miles down the river
An attractive young neighbor declared:

"There's a somethin' keeps bumpin' them willers.
There's a somethin' humped up in the brush.
You be brave an' hang on to your pillers.
Sleep along little darlins an' hush.

I'll be back when I've doubled the jinglers
On the stakes by the stormcellar door.
When them dead men feel that in their fingers
They jes' whimper an' head for the shore."

Light she ran with her housecoat a-flappin',
Where the waters was roilin' an' high.
There was somethin' a-waitin' to happen,
By the strobe-lighted look of the sky.

If you drift like a mist through the meadow,
If you curl to the edge of the draw,
You could nudge yourself up to a knothole,
But you might not believe what you saw.

On the bank where the crib and the shed ran
Hard aground in a Red River fling,
She is sprawled on the arm of a dead man,
And the dead man is startin' to sing:

"Roll me over my lovely my precious.
My migration has scarcely begun.
I can feel myself growing flotatious
To the wandering beams of the sun.

I can feel the old tug of the Delta
Where I drunk myself sick in my teens.
Roll me over. I suddenly felt a
Gnawful lot like a kid full of beans.

When the barns take a turn at the barn dance,
When the sheds start to thread through the trees,
I succumb to a superabundance
Of the Red River drifter's disease.

Give a kick to my side if you love me.
Cast me loose from this willowy slough.
There's a damn sight less dam site above me
And a damn sight less fuss and to-do.

Steer me out where the stars have arisen.
Point my head past the meadows downstream.
Hang a topsheet and main to the mizzen,
And I'd putt through the waves like a dream.

I can clear out the brush on the boundary.
I can clear out accounts at the store.
I can clear clear on out of the county
Like them hoboes and yokels of yore.

They can bury a box of the keepsakes
From my notable farming career.
They can deed what they need to them cheapskates
At the Farmers Supply in Grenier.

They can tell my twelve sons and my daughter
How I tended to take things too far,
Like the night I went down for some water
And ran off with the whole reservoir.

It's a sorrowful name I'm a-leaving.
It's a sorrowful sadness I feel.
If you get overwhelmed with the grieving
You can try this address in Mobile."

Now the neighbor is gone from the valley.
Now the flivver is out on display
In the Bonnie-and-Clyde grand finale
At the Wild-West Pavilion Café.

Now the widow reclines at the window
By the banks of the new reservoir.
On some shirts that the Sheriff come into
She embroiders a five-pointed star.

THE UNIVERSE IS
CLOSED AND HAS REMs

to Celia and Wally, to Milly and Gene

1.

One. one. one. one.
That's what God said.
Singular, singular, singular, singular,
Infinitely outspread.

Nothing under the nothing not even the sun.

No weight, no breadth, no negative, no north,
No three dimensions beckoning a fourth forth
With monumental pantomime, no buzz
Of energy-exchange, no instances.

It might have happened. Who knows which comes first,
The point flash, or some perfectly dispersed
Extrapolation into time-reversed
Of this explosion, this diaspora?

You like the God that freaks out and goes *"Unh!"*
I like the opposite extreme. How dull,
How uncollected, how bare-minimal
The necessary element might be.
One. one. one. Eternity.

Dead rudiments. None veer. None coalesce.

A pretty perpetuity unless —

Once one wants one twice two twice two the formalities take place.
Sub-elemental sarabandes objectify a space
Extravagantly sparse, and stilled, and stirless, but perhaps
Complicit. Something happening. Collapse.

2.

Absolute bash, and then

Sub-elemental smithereens again

But suddenly and picturesquely clotted
At every scale, down to the not-ness knotted
Into the nothing where a quark sleeps furious
And nags the smarmy noggins of the curious
With pointy-headed notions of the sphere
A quantum mass might shrink to, to cohere
Into its own black hole,
Inviolably sole
And satisfying to the theorist
Who likes his distillations with a twist
Of irreducibility at bottom.

Welcome to basic. Smoke 'em if you got 'em.
That does it for the first few trillion years.

Now then. If all you spacetime pioneers
'll dig into your briefing kits, behind
The replicative check sheet you should find
A rose-red pair of actuary googols
In case the credit mechanism boggles,
One windfall apple softened up with slug holes
To sniff at, and a parts list for these fogballs.
Mumble it to yourself if you get dizzy.
And hold tight. The next wiggle is a doozy.
Get used to it, 'cause you'll be getting lots o' these
Interchangeable pre-big-bang hypotheses.
And if the rose-red googols are a dud,
You bring it up at . . .

3. Question Period

Are we the first bounce, or the eightieth?

These dead immensities inventing death
Inventing difference inventing brilliance.
How many of them? Ten? A dozen? Trillions?

23

But if Xerxes
Had had Xeroxes . . .

If the aurochs
Got anthrax . . .

If the Mingel-Wurm
Returns . . .

No seriously. Look,
I mean I've read the book.
If having a trick thumb can tip the odds,
Why us-the-klutz? Why not cephalopods?
Put *brain* behind those graspings and completions,
Tune up those fine calcareous secretions
To gestate little lock-picks and escapements,
A quick squid'd run rings around these apemen's
Lathes and beams and hieroglyph prostheses
For busting big things down to byte-size pieces.
A thought could be the father to a stack
Of nacreous holography, played back
Instantly anywhere a clammy grip
Fondled the iridescent microchip.
And when it came to synthesizing sheer
Spectacle, to outface Poseidon's mere
Opulence and fecundity and scenery
With monuments of unaided Balanchinery —
Well — what I mean — why us?
Why not an offshoot of the octopus?

(If you knotted a cosmos.
If you twisted its wristwatch.
If you skidded it parsecs
In a picosec.)

But the Ik . . .
                                    The euglena . . .
                    The ozone . . .

4. Nap Time

Hush.

Everything in a minute. What's the rush?

24

It may work out. The big Let-there-be-light
May keep receding barely-out-of-sight.

Us prospectors can pan among the vestiges
With bright eyes and big dishes, nabbing hostages
But never quite contriving to decode
A backstairs access to the mother lode
That heaved up unimaginably once
And left this avalanche of evidence.
Awake, asleep, it streams right through our fingers.
Once in a blue moon, a neutrino lingers.
It drives these needle-in-the-haystack trackers
Crackers.

I like the latest inklings. Just this year
A theorist has posited a sheer
Propensity of Zilch to self-destruct.
That's what he says began it. That's what sucked
Somethingness out of Nothingness. Shazam.

ZILCH + ZILCH + NIL + NIL = NAUGHT

Cryptarithm in a puzzle book I bought.

I like the sense of *consequence*. Hot damn.

All this consequent middle. All this muddle.
Me the unlikely frog in so big a puddle
It puts the perfervid fancies of the priests
Back at about the level of a beast's
Diffuse imaginings of huger mangers
Where ever more companionable strangers
Scratch him behind the ears and pitch down food.

If only I could see how to preclude
Acting on every triggerable spin-off.

I can't. It's going to kill us, sure as gonif
And gizmo gravitate and groove.
The mills will grind; the merchandise will move.

I'm sorry Lennon died, but Lennon did.
What got him wasn't Belial-the-Kid.

25

Simple Possession loitered, and it pondered,
And found, until its concentration wandered,
a momentary sense of Rationale.

Recess time at the Okey-Doke Corral.

One possible response of the biota
Observable in front of the Dakota
Became the probable, since there was time.

Possession was nine-tenths of it, and I'm
Possessed. I have these Titans that I've paid for.
Polarises, Poseidons, Mark 12s made for
Me, and I haven't found a way to ditch 'em.

If I could tough it out like Robert Mitchum
And take the beating, confident the script
Would have me up, goof-balled and pistol-whipped
But standing, to choke back humiliation
And pick up the routine of my vocation
After the *big*-time baddies have their ball.

Not in the cards. We won't be here at all.
State-of-the-art has got way out ahead of us.

Dumb, then, for the merely not-yet-dead of us
To love the thing that kills us. But I do.

So beautiful, so various, so new.

Some times I want to bang their heads on the Universe and scream
"It's *beautiful*, you balmy bastards! THIS IS NOT A DREAM."

But no. I take my task as to record
At close hand, for the glory of no Lord,
Delight of no posterity, some part
Of what it was to take the world to heart
When all of it and more came flooding at us,
Absolutely positively gratis
And ravishing and perfectly disposed
To pal around with us an undisclosed
Number of million human generations
Until the Sun god goes on iron rations
And zaps us with a real survival crisis.

Wonderful: we just graduate from Isis
And Kali and Jehovah and all that
And start to see how hugely where-we're-at
Exceeds the psychedelic pipedreams of it,
And whammo.
              Tell the whole shebang I love it,
And buck the odds, and hope, and give it my
Borrowed scratched-up happy hello-goodbye.

THE STAUNCH MAID AND
THE EXTRATERRESTRIAL TREKKIE

hommages à Julia Child

Stand back stand back, Thou blob of
    jelly.
Do not attack
A maid so true.
I didn't pack
My Schiaparelli
To hit the sack
With a thang like you.

You maniac!
Go raid a deli.
Pick on a snack
Of barbecue.
A nice Cal-Jack?
Some Buoncastelli.
Here, have a daiq-
Uiri. Have two.

Like a Big-Mac
Machiavelli
She tossed him crack-
Ers and ragout.
She fed him rack
Of lamb, sowbelly,
Absinthe and cack-
Leberry stew.

And while she crack-
Ed the eggs and velly
Adroitly hack-
Ed the lamb in two,
Like that weird ac-
Tress on the telly,
Kept up a wack-
Y parlez-vous.

You shall not lack
For mortadelle.
You shall not lack
For pâte-à-choux.
You shall have aq-
Uavit quenelle
Mit sukiyak-
I au fondue.

But I must frac-
Ture the patellae
And baste the back-
Sides of a few
Agneaux-de-Pâques-
Avec-Mint-Jelly
Before I ac-
Quiesce to you.

Not yet you stack
Of parallelly
Pulsating vac-
Uoles of goo,
You sloshing brack-
Ish stracciatelli
Of dental plaque
And doggy doo!

I said back back!
Have Mrs. Shelley
Or Countess Drac-
Ula re-do
You you great hack-
Work by Fuseli.
I'm not the quack
To unscramble you.

28

She threw him mac-
Kerel en gelée,
Mulled Armagnac,
Ripe Danish blue.
She staggered back.
He swore by Hell he
Had come to shack
And not soft-shoe.

Just at the ac-
Me of Indeli-
Cacy and ac-
Rimony too,
While she distrac-
Ted him pellmellly,
The massed attack
Came in on cue:

Her Uncle Zack
From Pocatelly,
The whole *Galac-*
Tica and crew
On a Kawasak-
I-Granatelli-
Ford-Lotus trac-
Tor cab crashed through.

They had a tac
Nuke from New Delhi.
They had a black-
Snake from the zoo.
A few Kojak-
Eries from Telly.
Biff Bam Fppplt Thwack.
Poop poop a doo.

They hacked that frac-
Tious vermicelli
Till the tentac-
Ulations flew.
A rather tack-
Y, rather smelly
Business, but *chac-*
Un à son goût.

Without a knack
For belly-belly,
Without the ac-
Umen to do
Celeriac
Farcie Duxelle,
What would a crack-
Er damsel do?

SUNDAY BRUNCH IN THE
BOSTON RESTORATION

for George and Bab

1.

They've done it right by God: the historic spaces
stripped of their inauthentic accretions and made available
to the same dedicated commerce of far-fetched valuables
that got the whole Boston experience motating in the first place.

2.

This isn't just some godforsaken flier at a roadside small-business bonanza.
It's the embodied etiology of a mass hysterical daydream
worthy of one of the original merchant adventurers.

3.

And doesn't it strike you as extraordinary this practically teenage
Richelieu in the employ of the Proud Popover
ushering us up genuine Piranesian factory-style catwalk staircases
into the old stone echochambers of William Lloyd Garrison's thunder
thanks to the imaginativeness of the really great franchiser
who got him that frogged duck redcoat to hide his Anheuser
Busch Natural Light tee-shirt and beltbuckle under?

4.

Everybody a billboard! Certo! Chiapan or is it Belizian
floursackfacsimiles, Mazdamedallions, LeFigarologos
comparisonshopping the toveracks, the quarkbins, the
    wampeteropenerbarrels
right out in the openfront breakneck deafening cobble and rail and rubble
where Anthony Burns trudged and Vanzetti deliberated.

Whaddaya say we go crazy and buy us a cod.

5.

I'm coming, I'm coming, only a few small purchases.
But look at these little gizmos with the ceramic crankhandles.

30

6.

Find me the cheeses! Get me a melon! Buy me a lime!
Get me in ten-man tandem with them poets of the olden time
pillaging the quotidian, parceling it up into rhyme
and trucking it off the doorstep of posterity to deliver it
squalling righteous and barefaced like an Edward Everett.
It's beautiful, it's got character written all over it,
it's Boston even if a Bostonian has to discover it
hiding its mug where the mugracks flash the escutcheons
of ANTIOCK, AMHOIST, HANOVER AGRICULTURAL AND MECHANICAL,
and the pushcart piggybacks home on the Porsche-top ski-rack.

Toss me the big lyre and the Li Po clap-stick.
And if this ain't stuff enough for the metrical celebration
of spiritus loci, cold sliced pork pie and the celebrator's loquacity
while the harbor detail snap to and the snare drums roll,
then I have so misjudged mine and my L. L. Bean canvas tote bag's capacity
as to qualify for a hardship subscription to the Cosmopolitan.

7.

Get thee a heftier tote bag O my soul
we can open it wide and throw everything in we can call it an
Ode to the Boston of Zinn White Wojtyla Douglass Douglas Tubman and
      Martineau
we can open it wider and call down inside of it Rise up as one and be
      vocative O

baskets O briskets O bouquets O gourmet dishes
O rarebits and rice-boats, tikia-kebobs and shishes.
O microwave chicken Kiev O cashew quiches,
I am getting the hang of it, righthand-to-lefthand-lettered gefiltefishes,
weird little items for opening oysters. O knishes

O gjetost oh foozle it shouldn't be quiches it's quiches.
As in Gimme your Klimts, your Toulouses, your scenic Helvetias
and where is the waiter and where are our rock-cornishes flambées Grand-
      Corniches
and what do they do for an encore, these fabulous groomed-to-the-eyeballs
      geishas
steering their highstrung miniatures on scissoring leashes

from the Parker House to Felicia's I mean Feli-, uh, Felicia's
by way of the two-buck prawns and the 3-lb. peaches
of Quincy Market and Haymarket market O sakes O pulques O chichas
oh foozle again I keep running aground on these rhapsodological beaches

where as soon as you say geishas you wish you could take it back and say
    geishas
but too late! too late! they go vanishing under the feathery glassed-in
    acacias
looking as ravishingly underdeveloped as Sam Jaffe's or J. Carroll Naish's
MittelShangrilavian accent when they used to come on after the *Ars Gratia*s

but look! handpainted Haitian creches I mean creches
but look! ravaging tandems of pitilessly nubile Arapeshes

closing on us like a full-court press-gang for the La Leches I'm sorry La
    Leches,
their Chés, turquoise-on-pink, vivid against giant four-color display Chés
and the vocables won't sit still it's like one of the W.H.A.'s
amateur-nights-on-ice it's like maybe it's something I ate chez

O'Dea's maybe it's pardon me lady that cafe chaise pardon me cafe chaise
longue I am fainting a little don't tell me I know it it shouldn't be J. Carroll
    Naish's

pitheco-Indo-European it shoulda been J. Carroll plain old Naish's
as in On second thought we'll settle for two corned beef hashes
and a cup of joe
and a quick ticket to Nantasket or Squibnocket or Îlot-au-Haut
because as a Nash from the great days of the Nashes might've lamented, O
it isn't the cuisinart it's the cuisine argot
and I don't care if it's the argot as in the argot merchant disaster
or the argot as in What kindsa colada makings the bar got
or all three
simultaneously
as in the American Heritage Dictionary of the English Language
which is about as much help on the point as a set of chopsticks with a hero
    sandwich
but at least lends the entire weight of its authority to the inherent confusion
while the ode goes marching along without me to its conclusion
twirling its objects methodically while the rhymes keep ranks
in spite of an occasional brownbagger or Pomeranian nipping at its flanks
and holy Ned. Like Nantucket said to the Argo's hapless master
Good-bye, Captain Papadopoulos, and thanks.

SONNET IN THE SHAPE OF A POTTED CHRISTMAS TREE

*

O
fury-
bedecked!
O glitter-torn!
Let the wild wind erect
bonbonbonanzas; junipers affect
frostyfreeze turbans; iciclestuff adorn
all cuckolded creation in a madcap crown of horn!
It's a new day; no scapegrace of a sect
tidying up the ashtrays playing Daughter-in-Law Elect;
bells! bibelots! popsicle cigars! shatter the glassware! a son born
now
now
while ox and ass and infant lie
together as poor creatures will
and tears of her exertion still
cling in the spent girl's eye
and a great firework in the sky
drifts to the western hill.

POEMS FROM THE 1950s,
FROM THE BOOK **BONE THOUGHTS**

KIDSTUFF
AND
SWITCHBOARDS II.

WAR STORY

The 4th of July he stormed a nest.
He won a ribbon but lost his chest.
We threw his arms across the rest
    And kneed him in the chin.
    (You knee them in the chin
    To drive the dog-tag in.)

The 5th of July the Chaplain wrote.
It wasn't much; I needn't quote.
The widow lay on her davenport
    Letting the news sink in.
    (Since April she had been
    Letting the news sink in.)

The 6th of July the Captain stank.
They had us pinned from either flank.
With all respect to the dead and rank
    We wished he was dug in.
    (I mean to save your skin
    It says to get dug in.)

The word when it came was nine days old.
Lieutenant Jones brought marigolds.
The widow got out the Captain's Olds
    And took him for a spin.
    (A faster-than-ever spin:
    Down to the Lake, and in.)

A TAPESTRY FOR BAYEUX

I. *Recto*

Over the
  seaworthy
cavalry
  arches a
rocketry
  wickerwork:
involute
  laceries
lacerate
  indigo
altitudes,
  making a
skywritten

filigree
  into which,
lazily,
  LCTs
sinuate,
  adjutants
next to them
  eversharp-
eyed, among
  delicate
battleship
  umbrages
twinkling an

anger as
  measured as
organdy.
  Normandy
knitted the
  eyelets and
yarn of these
  warriors'
armoring —
  ringbolt and

dungaree,
    cable and
axletree,

tanktrack and
    ammobelt
linking and
    opening
garlands and
    islands of
seafoam and
    sergeantry.
Opulent
    fretwork: on
turquoise and
    emerald,
red instants

accenting
    neatly a
dearth of red.
    Gunstations
issue it;
    vaportrails
ease into
    smoke from it —
yellow and
    ochre and
umber and
    sable and
out. Or that

man at the
    edge of the
tapestry
    holding his
inches of
    niggardly
ground and his
    trumpery
order of
    red and his
equipage
    angled and

dated. He.

II. *Verso*

Wasting no
   energy,
Time, the old
   registrar,
evenly
   adds to his
scrolls, rolling
   up in them
rampage and
   echo and
hush — in each
   influx of
surf, in each

tumble of
   raincloud at
evening,
   action of
seaswell and
   undertow
rounding an
   introvert
edge to the
   surge until,
manhandled
   over, all
surfaces,

tapestries,
   entities
veer from the
   eye like those
rings of lost
   yesteryears
pooled in the
   oak of your
memory.
   Item: one
Normandy
   Exercise.

Muscle it

over: an
    underside
rises: a
    raggedy
elegant
    mess of an
abstract: a
    rip-out of
kidstuff and
    switchboards, where
amputee
    radio
elements,

unattached
    nervefibre
conduits,
    openmouthed
ureters,
    tag ends of
hamstring and
    outrigging
ripped from their
    unions and
nexuses
    jumble with
undeterred

speakingtubes
    twittering
orders as
    random and
angry as
    ddt'd
hornets. Step
    over a
moment: peer
    in through this
nutshell of
    eyeball and
man your gun.

NAMED INDIVIDUAL

They hold the committee today.
Today they get to me.
I wasn't invited. They say
the public gets in free.

The man I have this from
wouldn't divulge his face.
I heard, in the dead hum
that took his voice's place,

something I almost hear
in you. (You purse your eyes,
look from ear to ear
and back again.) Surmise

a room, the table set
with fists, the fists with sheaves
of evidence as yet
safe in manila sleeves.

Suppose commercials done,
cameras, papers, fists
set moving, everyone
plunged in light to the wrists.

Say, when those hands aghast,
those thumbs awag with woe,
jig like the naked cast
of a Punch and Judy show,

that pretty comedy
draws millions. Say they gawk
too openmouthed for glee,
too tranquilized for shock.

Say every well-fed gut
unshaken at that jape

eases or freezes shut
one stronghold of escape

and every head that smiles
in torpor or assent
nods me the empty miles
of its imprisonment . . .

But say I came to *you,*
waiting for you to speak?
Would I be such a jew?
Am I so damned unique?

Surely there are a few —
well —
friends that I could seek?

UNFRIENDLY WITNESS

I never played the Moor,
I never looked to see,
I don't know what my hands are for,
I know they're not for me:

I lent them to my Mother,
she yanked them into rules
and put them with my pencilbox
as fit to take to school;

I lent them to my Teacher,
she ruled them into pens
and sent them home to Fatherdear
who beat them straight again;

I lent them to my Judge,
he penned them into line,
since when they clasp and hold I swear
nothing of yours, or mine;

I lent them to my Sergeant,
he lined them into squads
and marched them off to sudden death
like little piston rods;

Death sent them back unused,
I squandered them on love:
they took the world for comrade then
as easy as a glove.

And yet the world is heavy
and filled with men like me —
with tired men, with heavy men
that slip my memory
if that be perjury.

COMMUNICATION TO
THE CITY FATHERS OF BOSTON

Dear Sirs: Is it not time we formed a Boston
Committee to Enact a Dirge for Boston?

When the twelve-minute countdown comes, when Boston's
people convened in unaccustomed basements
feel on their necks the spiderwebs of bombsights,
when subway stations clot and fill like beesnests
making a honey-heavy moan, whose business
will it be then to mourn, to take a busman's
holiday from his death, to weep for Boston's?

Though dust is scattered to her bones, though grieving
thunderheads add hot tears, though copper grapevines
clickety-clack their telegraphic ragtime
tongues at the pity of it, how in God's name
will Boston in the thick of Armageddon
summon composure to compose a grave-song
grand and austere enough for such a grieving?

Move we commit some song, now, to the HOLD files
of papers in exotic places. Helpful
of course to cram some young ones with hogs' headfuls
of Lowells, khaki-cap them, ship them wholesale
out. There's a chance, in one of them the hairsbreadth
imminence of the thing may speak. But Hell's fire,
what'll they have on us in all those HOLD files?

You want some rewrite man to wrap up Boston
like garbage in old newsprint for the dustbin?
The Statehouse men convivial at Blinstrub's,
the textile men, the men of subtler substance
squiring Ledaean daughters to the swan-boats,
the dockers, truckers, teenage hotrod-bandits —
what could he make of them, to make them Boston?

Or even make of me, perched in these Park Street
offices playing Jonah like an upstart

45

pipsqueak in raven's clothing — First Mate Starbuck
who thinks too much? Thinking of kids in bookstores
digging for dirty footnotes to their Shakespeares,
while by my window the Archbishop's upstairs
loudspeaker booms redemption over Park Street.

Thinking of up the hill the gilded Statehouse
where just last night the plaster-of-paris faces
of Sacco and Vanzetti craned on flannel
arms at the conscientiously empaneled
pain of a state's relentlessly belated
questioning of itself. (Last year the Salem
Witches; next year, if next year finds a Statehouse . . . ?)

Thinking of Thor, Zeus, Atlas. Thinking Boston.
Thinking there must be words her weathered brownstone
could still re-whisper — words to blast the brassbound
brandishers on their pads — words John Jay Chapman
scored on her singlehanded — words Sam Adams,
Garrison, Mott, Thoreau blazed in this has-been
Braintree-Jamaica-Concord-Cambridge-Boston.

There were such men. Or why remember Boston?
All of them dead of course. Or else old Boston
wouldn't be acting like a perfect Boston,
counting its thumbs and counting up the Boston
dividend-factors in this made-in-Boston
guidance-umbrella heisted over Boston
leaking the gods' own laughter in on Boston

while the apprentice ironists of Boston
target the obvious. But then that's Boston.

CORA PUNCTUATED
WITH STRAWBERRIES

Sandra and that boy that's going to get her in trouble
one of these days were out in the garden where anyone in
Mother's sickroom could see them out the upperleft corner of the
window sitting behind the garage feeding each other
blueberries and Cherry was helping with the dishes alone in the
kitchen and
um good strawberries if we did grow them just can't can without
popping one in every so often Henry was at it again in the
attic with that whatchamacallit of his when the Big
Bomb fell smack in the MacDonalds' yard you know over on
Elm and they got into Life and the papers and all all very
well but they might have been in when it hit and it would have
been a very different story for Lucy MacDonald then I'll tell
you well they say it was right in the Geographic Center of the
country the Geographic
woody Center you could hear it just as plain I thought the
elevator had blown up and I guess you read yourself the awful
things it would have
ik another one woody I tell you I don't know what's got
into these strawberries used to be so juicy they
say they only had the one and it's all it would have took well I
always knew we could beat the enemy they made such
shoddy tricks and spring-toys and puzzles and fuses and
things and besides, it wouldn't have been right.

IF SATURDAY

Four easy hours from San Francisco, yes
the sitting mallards tip like steel-plate ducks.
Among them, clay-pipe fishes leap and pop
before your eyes, before your eyes are there.
As advertised, these mountains cool their claws
and show their sleepless nerves merely as trees:
no crossed gray crosses scratch against the sky.
A frequency of birds pick out a channel,
make their plain statement, fade it into blue.
Lay out your arms like rods on the calm water,
clench and extend your tackle, float it gently
above green fish that measurelessly tread
the green plush colonnades of an obscure
courtiership. Your marriage is this moment.
Great arcs of pine and geese complete your sphere.

Two easy voices and a boat from now,
this soon the evening Limited of wind
at distant crossings laying dismal sounds,
the sun comes to your level like a friend.
Dying a friend, it leaks away, unhurried
as a man of time . . . But what upstart humps
in with a sun grin at the deathbed's left —
what idiot Announcer — what Late Flash?
whose ripe orange orb of power, risen, rots —
holes in your eyes too deep, too black for water.
The bomb. Who would have thought. The bomb. But there
the bastions rise until the capstone's on
that tipping monolith of cloud; and now
as ever a south-flying mallard swings
like any late commuter to the moving
platform of the warping, wooden water.

The trees fall singly into dark formation.
You, with your untried gun, inherit all.
Down in the valleys, dust rain will be falling
and leaning masts above suburban dwellings
claw empty pictures from the breeding air.

48

And you, with your lines dry, inherit all.
Row to the shore. The bomb. The bomb, the bastards.
Tell it, the two of you. Say until morning.
Say till the world retakes its age-old shapes,
lifting again the green receiving branches
eight easy minutes from the sun. The roads
will have their fill awhile of flesh in motion,
mindlessly nerved to murder as it dies.
Nations convulsing, their great thought gone static,
try your mere voices; try small work of hands.
One must begin by helping one; and you,
best-armed of pioneers, most learned savage,
granted a day's north wind, inherit all.

NEW STRAIN

You should see these musical mice.
   When we start the device
they rise on their haunches and sniff
   the air as if
they remembered all about dancing.
   Soon they are chancing
a step or two, and a turn.
   How quickly they learn
the rest, and with leaps and spins
   master the ins
and outs of it, round and round
   and round. We found
the loudest music best
   and now we test
with a kind of electric bell
   which works as well.

In two to two-and-a-quarter
   minutes, a shorter
rhythm captures the front
   legs, and they stunt
in somersaults until
   they become still
and seem to have lost their breath.
   But the sign of death
is later: the ears, which have been
   flat, like a skin
skullcap, relax and flare
   as if the air
might hold some further thing
   for the listening.

COLD-WAR BULLETIN
FROM THE CULTURAL FRONT

The proposed new U.S. Consulate at Algiers
will be an ultra-modern structure . . . described
by the architects as "a feast of great low glass
domes."

We're building a building
in functional glass
at Algiers in Algeria:
no gargoyles, no gilding,
none of your crass
classic criteria:
one functional mass
of glass —

glass fibre, glass block,
glass fenestration,
with cut-glass tears
on the chandeliers
and pier-glass piers
clear to bedrock
(not far at Algiers)
for foundation.

But if domes of glass
of critical area
tend to let pass
units of mass,
heat, or hysteria,
we can gild with gilding
our functional building
in Algeria:

sun will not pierce
a glare so fierce,
and we'll station stations
of heads-of-legation
all round the block
with anti-rock rocks
(and anti-jeer jeers)
at Algiers.

51

CHICAGO, CHICAGO

1.

April. The City, wrapped
in unaccustomed grace,
goes scarlet where they slapped
a garden in her face.
Still working at the place
she found her rotten set
of ivory towers gapped
when the last fair pulled out.

We head out for the park
from Iris and Rose's bar.
Watching the dancers bare
their little almost-all,
letting the whiskey work,
lusty and lachrymal,
has primed us: it's not far:
it might as well befall.

2.

The elms along the drag
have shuffled into shag-
dance action, like the hag
of husks and crumbs, awag
triumphantly above
the feeding frenzy of
the pigeon and the dove
and the wee chipmunk, Love.

Bare ruined chorus-lines,
for what they are, they stand.
the winoes give them a hand.
Where amber light refines
a canopy of flowers
to wax, it may be hours

before a prowlcar shines
and pounces.
                 Understand? —

                 we didn't come to Walt's,
                 we didn't come to Dan's,
                 we come to Rose and Iris's,
                 Iris's, man.

                 Their shapes may be piracies,
                 their colors may be false,
                 but you know you've seen a dance
                 when they shake that schmaltz.

3.

Winds of morning sift
down through the heavy wires
and branches like a gift
of tongues. Our voices drift
lazily on a wash
of motors, brushes, tires —
street-cleaning — the soft flush
of a cat-house after hours.

We'll make it: worlds of time:
even the winoes seem
posted to see us home;
and shoring up the elms,
shoring up the el,
lighting up an L & M
butt, they serve as well
as any sentinel.

4.

Behind us, the gates lock.
The iron rolling-stock
of the bankrupt CTA
jolts, and gets underway.
This is the only Rock:
give with your knees, and sway

53

close to the very wreck
they had here yesterday.

Back of the yellowed laces
flaunting past our faces,
the usual embraces
turn sacred and are sped.
With some who will curse bread,
with some who will free races,
her majesty replaces
its defeated dead.

AB OVO

Beak gumming my entrails,
wings elbowing my temples,
there's this bird wants out.

Suppose I just let crack,
and he rolls out the red neck,
gets balanced on one foot?

If he bows a backward knee,
if he stands there woodenly,
is this a dove, or what?

I mean he'll be all moist,
liquid-tongued, not voiced,
with wattles on his throat.

Honey, in a word,
this hotshot headlong bird
Love is a strange coot.

BONE THOUGHTS
ON A DRY DAY

Walking to the museum
over the Outer Drive,
I think, before I see them
dead, of the bones alive.

I think of how the snake smoothed over the fact,
but hung sharp beads around its charmer's neck.

The jawbone of my cat.
So easily held shut.
Breakable as ice.

Mice.

The mouse of course is a berry, his bones mere seeds.
Step on him once and see.

You mustn't think that the fish
choke on those bones, or that chickens wish.

Chickens
pedaling like the dickens,
getting away on a five-man tandem bike,
unlike
that legless headstrong showoff on crutches, the ostrich.

Only the skull of a man makes much of an ashtray.

Whereas the wise old bat
dumps his bones in a bag
and hangs it on a hook,

the elephant says look
how I can put

this on top of that.

Here's a conundrum.
Tug of a toe, blunt-bowed barge of a thighbone,
gondola-squadron of ribs, and the jaw scow.

Carried along somehow,
keeping our eyes peeled
for what we were just yesterday,
we surge into the Field
Museum of Natural History
with busloads full of kids.

Whole-hog hominids.

FABLE FOR
BLACKBOARD

Here is the grackle, people.
Here is the fox, folks.
The grackle sits in the bracken. The fox
    hopes.

Here are the fronds, friends,
that cover the fox.
The fronds get in a frenzy. The grackle
    looks.

Here are the ticks, tykes,
that live in the leaves, loves.
The fox is confounded,
and God is above.

TECHNOLOGIES

On Commonwealth, on Marlborough,
the gull beaks of magnolia
were straining upward like the flocks
harnessed by kings in storybooks
who lusted for the moon. Six days
we mooned into each other's eyes
mythologies of dune and dawn.

They do the trick with rockets now.
With methodologies of steel.
With industry or not at all.
What does it come to? Ask the trees
carrying out their lunacies
for all they are, for all they know
on Commonwealth, on Marlborough.

ON FIRST LOOKING IN ON
BLODGETT'S *KEATS'S "CHAPMAN'S HOMER"*
(*Summer.* ½ credit. Monday 9–11)

Mellifluous as bees, these brittle men
droning of Honeyed Homer give me hives.
I scratch, yawn like a bear, my arm arrives
at yours — oh, Honey, and we're back again,
me the Balboa, you the Darien,
lording the loud Pacific sands, our lives
as hazarded as when a petrel dives
to yank the dull sea's coverlet, or when,

breaking from me across the sand that's rink
and record of our weekend boning up
on *The Romantic Agony,* you sink
John Keats a good surf-fisher's cast out — plump
in the sun's wake — and the parched pages drink
that great whales' blanket party hump and hump.

1958:
POEMS FROM A FIRST YEAR IN BOSTON

1. Hospital Visits. Visits to Beacon Hill.

Boston. Lord God the ocean never to windward,
never the sweet snootful of death a West Coast
wind on its seven-league sea-legs winds its wing-ding
landfalling up by upheaving over you.
                              Winedark
hunger for some washboard music to this one-way
maze.
        Hunger for the stink of kelp winrowed
on beaches. Hunger for the hills, hills somewhere
anchoring the dizzy sky. No wonder
it groans, groans. It's the wind's own girl I waylaid
through deserts who sours here, a sick wife.
                              With land-wind.
Nothing but land-wind hot with steel, but lint-white
bundles of daily breath hung out over textile
towns, but the sweat sucked from mines, white smokestacks
soaring from hospital workyards over grassplots
of pottering dotards. Take it, the dead wind whispers,
crouch to its weight: three thousand miles, three hundreds-
of-years of life rolled up in a wind, rolled backwards
onto this city's back, Jonathan Edwards.

Funny old crank of social history lectures,
firm believer in hell and witches, who knows whether
you of all witnesses wouldn't watch this wayward
city with most love?
                    And the busy winter
bustle of steam and batting. And the white-wound
handiwork of the nurses, the spattered internes
sober as bloody judges, culling the downtown
haul of the mercy fleet, while rearing and sounding
through panicked traffic the sacred scows come horns-down
heaping the hecatomb. The pretty hundreds
of bells nod off to sleep like practiced husbands
propped in high corners of their lady Boston's

white-laid and darkened room.
                              And yachtsmen, footloose
legatees fitting reefers into faultless
features with febrile wrists, protest: some leftist
restlessness threatens them in brittle leaflets;
some angry boy, some undiscovered artist
has put soot whiskers on their public statues.
They wring their strange left hands that every-whichways
scatter the khakied corpses onto elsewhere's
turbulent waters to save oil. Peer westward
plotting the last-ditch sally of The West.
Peer from the Free World's keep.
                              Old pioneer,
Jonathan Edwards, did you stop off here
where marsh-birds skittered, and a longboat put
its weed-grown bones to pasture at the foot
of Beacon, close on Charles Street? And see then,
already sick with glut, this hill of men?
And even there, see God? And in this marsh,
and in the wood beyond, grace of a harsh
God? And in these crabbed streets, unto the mid-
mire of them, God? Old Soul, you said you did.

2. Jack Spicer Says There Is No Witchcraft in Boston

What's with the shrub rubbish? I'd say it's witchcraft.
Brats in the belfries, catboats in the outskirts,
junk maples at the dump sites waving kerchiefs,
something there is, it sure ain't Spring yet, itches
to kick this customary blacktop dragster
into a new gear. In a quick-march mischief
her prim white picture-postcard patchwork
slithers on down the Charles. The crisscrossed Mystic
twitches in snazzy sequins though the calls
of her small tugs entice no geese. All's
up; all's on us; a life raft wakens the waters
of Walden like a butt-slap.
                              And yet she loiters.
Where's for-keeps while the lark in winter quarters
lolls? What's to solace Scollay's hashhouse floaters
and sing them to their dolls? and yet —
                              strange musics,
migrant melodies of exotic ozarks,

61

twitter and throb where the bubble-throated jukebox
lurks iridescent by these lurid newsracks.
Browser leafing here, withhold your wisecracks:
tonight, in public, straight from overseas,
her garish chiaroscuro turned to please
you and her other newsstand devotees,
the quarter-lit Diana takes her ease.

So watch your pockets, cats, hang on to your hearts,
for when you've drunk her glitter till it hurts —
Curtain.
          Winds frisk you to the bone.
                            Full-feasted
Spring, like an ill bird, settles to the masthead
of here and there an elm. The streets are misted.
A Boston rain, archaic and monastic,
cobbles the blacktop waters, brings mosaic
to dusty windshields; to the waking, music.

3. Surfeit and Hot Sleep

Heavy on branch, on tight green knuckles heaves
the Spring. Cumulus, thick as broodhens, thieves
green from the earthy bark like worms, like leaves,
like dollars from up sleeves.
                         Outbreak of billfolds,
bellbottoms, burleycue babes. Musical billboards
join the parade. And deep in bars the railbirds
listen: "They selling something?" "Can't tell, traffic."
On corners cats bounce once or twice: "Hey frantic."
"Yeah." and they stop. Flared forward like an intake
the lips lurch on. DISASTER OUTLET, NATICK
BEHEMOTH BARGAINS MONSTER DEALS TITANIC
the soundtruck reads; but what it says is "Mine.
You're my obsession. No I can't resign
possession. I'm confessin' that you're mine
mine mine mine mine click." Da Capo. Move on.

Slowly the moon, that shifty chaperone,
performs her preconcerted wink. Green, green
upon green, hips the store windows — I mean
it's summer now, that lolloping large mother,
comes puttering about some spell or other

among her brats the beasts.
                              And milky mutter
of pigeons, splash of children, scissoring shadows
weave us asleep as if there were no goddess
other than this of love, as if old Venus,
sprawled on the Common grass, her honeyed wonder's
hernia'd ruiner snoozing against her shoulder,
had found a better nature with an older.

There's something still goes on on Beacon's backstairs,
there's something gets discovered in the drugstores,
but it's not hers, not Cupid's, not the Dog Star's.
The prank still plays, but it's a colder jokester's.

If spring and fall and all, the hapless hustler
does her impersonation of the picture-
palace posture on an Elvis poster,
if spring and fall and all, her helter-skelter
sisters go squealing to the marriage-smelter,
the tin-pan Moon, the Moon's to blame!
                                        Throngs
follow the bouncing ball and sing along,
singing about the Moon in every song,
singing about the Moonbeam scoobie-doo,
Using the Moon to slouch allegiance to —

A pox!
        Powder with stardust. While the bride's
the broad's the broodmare's Moon at a cloud's side
poses and slowly the light is hers. She glides,
golden, an apple of eyes, and so cold, only
heart at its heaviest can join the lonely
circle in emptiness that is her dance.
Yet she is Love, our Love, that frantic cadence.

Gasp at the flash fadeaway into the dot
that swallows the bright stridency of the sign-off shot.
Shuddering just to think it, think with what
aplomb the proud haunch of the Moon hangs through,
while far back in the dark she truckles to,
stoppling her champagne giggles, what rough crew

WHAT WORKS

(An admired *ko-an* of the Zen Buddhists goes
as follows: *There is a live goose in a bottle.
How does one remove the goose without hurt-
ing it or damaging the bottle?* An admired an-
swer is: *Behold, I have done it!* John Holmes's
poem "Poetry Defined" settled the matter thus,
in its last lines:
          I put it in with my words.
          I took it out the same way.
          And what worked with these
          Can work with any words I say.)

I had a lovely bottle, bottle-blue
in color with a heavy bottle-shape.
It filled my kitchen table (window too)
as round, as fine, as dusty as a grape,
but not as edible.
                    Reading my friend
John Holmes's poem "Poetry Defined;
or a Short Course in Goose-Bottling by Mind-
Over-Matter," I smiled: I saw an end
to certain problems. Yes, a goose would serve.

Laying out axe and pot, steeling my nerve,
"Doggone, I've put this goose in this-here bottle,"
I said. And it worked: there she was — a beaut! all
white and afraid. Now:
              "There she is!" I cried.
Thunk went the fatted shoulders. Well, she tried.
"There she is!" *Thunk.* "THERE she is!"
                     What the heck,
they came out, goose and bottle, neck and neck
each time. Seizing the pot-lid, *Thwack!* My eyes
buzzed as the blue-green bits like sizzling flies
diamond-drilled them. Oh, if words could show them:
fires, flares, rockets, the works! *There* was a poem!
(spent like a wish, of course, after one use)
but here, Kind Reader, here is our bruised goose.

III.

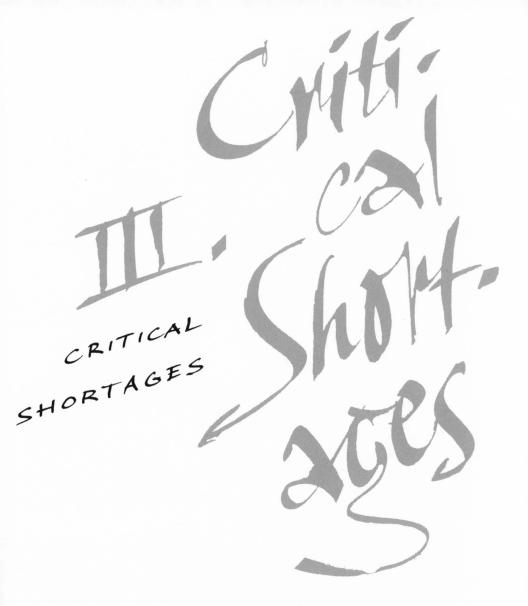

CRITICAL SHORTAGES

POEMS FROM THE 1960s,
FROM THE BOOK **WHITE PAPER**

FOR AN AMERICAN BURIAL

for Doris, for John

Slowly out of the dust-bedeviled air,
and off the passing blades of the gang plow,
and suddenly in state, as here and now,
the earth gathers the earth. The earth is fair;
all that the earth demands is the earth's share;
all we embrace and revel in and vow
never to lose, always to hold somehow,
we hold of earth, in temporary care.

Baby the sun goes up the sun goes down,
the roads turn into rivers under your wheels,
houses go spinning by, the lights of town
scatter and close, a galaxy unreels,
this endlessness, this readiness to drown,
this is the death he stood off, how it feels.

THE STARRY NIGHT

Faraway hands are folded and folded
or pick at the threads in the lap of blackness
or spool and spool at the tenantless tangle
of blackness, of blackness, of emptiness.

They are the stars; you can see them flash
like the bonewhite fingers of finicky ladies;
and far and away the depth of their cunning
is distance: a tissue of distances.

Their heads are down, they are plummeting downward,
we cling to our millwheel meadows, their heads
are bowed to the task: no comet commotion
of gazes effaces the emptiness.

On the rest-home porches at paranoid random
great-aunt and great-grandmother jaw like fates
till we wish them to heaven. They give us our wishes.
We cling to the earth and each other. They

take their place at the nets of blackness,
take their place at the great sea wall:
the mending, the mending, the never-mending
of blackness, of blackness, of emptiness.

OF LATE

"Stephen Smith, University of Iowa sophomore, burned what he said was
    his draft card"
and Norman Morrison, Quaker, of Baltimore Maryland, burned what he
    said was himself.
You, Robert McNamara, burned what you said was a concentration
of the Enemy Aggressor.
No news medium troubled to put it in quotes.

And Norman Morrison, Quaker, of Baltimore Maryland, burned what he
    said was himself.
He said it with simple materials such as would be found in your kitchen.
In your office you were informed.
Reporters got cracking frantically on the mental disturbance angle.
So far nothing turns up.

Norman Morrison, Quaker, of Baltimore Maryland, burned, and while
    burning, screamed.
No tip-off. No release.
Nothing to quote, to manage to put in quotes.
Pity the unaccustomed hesitance of the newspaper editorialists.
Pity the press photographers, not called.

Norman Morrison, Quaker, of Baltimore Maryland, burned and was
    burned and said
all that there is to say in that language.
Twice what is said in yours.
It is a strange sect, Mr. McNamara, under advice to try
the whole of a thought in silence, and to oneself.

A SONNET FROM 1965

Your poem is issued to you so
you may burn it and so
it may cost you burning and so
it is issued to you. Burn it.

Perhaps no more than a draft
will have as yet been issued.
There have been critical shortages.
Honor the draft and burn it.

Perhaps in your case only
a symbol is issued pending
the draft, pending completion
of the true poem. Burn it.

Maybe someone hands
you a burning issue. Burn it.

DEAR FELLOW TEACHER

I must confess I'm tired of these demonstrations.
Surely there must be better demonstrations
against brute force than brute force demonstrations.
Come now and let us reason together like
the Old Man says. What kind of a demonstration
is this from academically trained minds?
Is a stalled freight our cogent demonstration?
Is a blocked highway where some unwashed mob
panics at a mere word like "napalm" our
idea of perspicacious demonstration?
Would Aristotle, master of demonstration,
have dignified with the proud name "demonstration"
this massing of dumb bodies under flags?
Would Euclid have admired such demonstration?

What are we after with these demonstrations?
Accommodation? Compromise? Then let
that spirit permeate our demonstrations.
Was it not Secretary Rusk who said
We have already made our demonstration
of readiness to negotiate unquote?
What could be more amenable than that?
And had we not in fact for five whole days
called off, forsworn, and utterly regrouped
(for that is how we made said demonstration)
our prior and like-minded demonstration
of readiness to negotiate unquote?
Were we discouraged? Did we not resume
what McNamara calls our demonstration

that we shall not be bluffed or made to yield
until, in Bundy's words, some demonstration
of comparable etcetera unquote?
Lyndon, I'm sick and tired of demonstrations.
There is a demon in these demonstrations.
I'm fed up with the mere word "demonstration."
Furthermore, I accept your demonstration
that this or that or any demonstration's

about as much use a plugged piastre.
Like alibis, like sides of beef on spits,
like children in thatch villages of huts,
if you don't watch them they get overdone.
That's the damn thing about these demonstrations.
Let's everybody go out and stop one.

PIT VIPER

A slow burn
in cold blood
is all snake
muscle does.
The nerves drone
their dull red
test pattern
for days. Days.

The eyes, black
pushbuttons,
are just that.
On each side
a fixed dish
antenna
covers the
infrared.

The ribs, like
a good set
of stiff twin
calipers,
lie easy
and don't take
measure of
what's not there.

The skin's dim
computer-
controlboard
arrangement
of massed lights
displays no
waste motion.
Take no joy.

A strike force
is no more
than its parts
but these parts
work. Dead-game
defensework
specialists,
they die well.

The point is
they don't choose
livings: they
don't choose Death.
God save them
they aren't small-
time haters
that joined up.

BUT THAT I HAVE BAD DREAMS

Not the obscene beefiness of the fenceposts holds him,
but the exquisiteness of the barbed wire.
A late Vogue model casually centerfolds him
over her shoulder and carts him into the fire
ceaselessly accomplishing the purification of Buchenwald.
His sleep mask is upon him, he guzzles flame like a scalding brine,
and this and its freight of dead, the tallowed and hair-stuck bones, is called
Scheme of the Dream Devoutly to Be Dreamt, Study Nine.

He is my highschool English teacher Mr. Sales,
late chief of a J.A.G. Graves-registration team.
It is 1946. This night again he fails
and swirls in the old white rapids, the only dream:
dusk at the Pullman window — cloudscape fading — the wires astream —
convulvulate once more with nightingales.

THE DEPOSITION

His mouth hangs like a socket from which some noise
appropriate to it has been disconnected.
Evidence of real violence flakes from his working cheek
like dried hot chocolate.
Whatever he's been through these didn't do it.
The desk sergeant leaning forward looks merely sick,
and the kid back from the corner with coffee for the boys
just ill-complected.

There is no malice in the detective lieutenant's frown,
nor ugliness in the way his fellow officer
shoulders deponent's weight by means of deponent's arm:
nothing here to alarm
the hastily summoned License Bureau stenographer
who kneels, straining to follow, taking him down.

LATE LATE

Where tomahawks flash in the powwow
and tommyguns deepen the hubbub
and panzers patrol, is the horror
I live without sleep for the love of,

whose A-bombs respond to the tom-tom,
whose halberds react to the ack-ack,
while I, as if slugged with a dumdum,
sit back and sit back and sit back

until the last gunman is drawn on,
last murderous rustler druv loco,
last prisoncamp commandant spat at,
and somehow, and poco a poco,

the bottles are gone from the sixpack,
sensation is gone from the buttocks,
Old Glory dissolves into static,
the box is a box is a box.

THE WELL-TRAINED
ENGLISH CRITIC SURVEYS
THE AMERICAN SCENE

"Poetic theory in America is at present in an
extremely curious state, resembling that of Eng-
land during the Barons' Wars rather than that
of a healthy democracy or well-run autocracy.
It is not even a decent civil war . . ."
— THOM GUNN in *Yale Review*

Sometimes I feel like a fodderless cannon
On one of those midwestern courthouse lawns
Fiercely contested for by boys of ten and
Topped by a brevet general in bronze.

Hallucination, naturally: no
Era without its war, and this has its,
Roundabout somewhere, some imbroglio,
Even if only run by starts and fits.

Limber me up again, somebody.
In with the charges! To the touch-hole! Wham!
Elevate me, ignite me, let one ruddy
Side or the other taste the thing I am!

This pale palaver, this mish-mash of factions:
How can you find employment in a war
Of private sorties and guerrilla actions?
Maddening! Maddening! It chokes the bore!

Great God why was I tempered of pure sheffield
Unless to belch and fulminate and reek?
Never in England would I be so stifled.
Name me the nearest caitiff: let me speak!

I DREAMT I WENT
SHOOTING FISH
IN MY BARE CHEST

"When I shoot fish I don't wear an AquaLung
— it evens out the odds."
                    — IAN FLEMING, quoted in *Life*

I never shoot fish in an AquaLung.
    It might unbalance the odds.
I give the sucker an even break —
The sucker the snapper the grouper the hake
    And suitable cephalopods.
I'm not cast iron: I sometimes quake
    As I stalk with my weapon unslung;
But all advantage I deign to take
Is a love of danger for danger's sake
    And a knack with heaters and rods
        A certain
    Knack with heaters and rods.

I never shoot fish in an AquaLung.
    The man who would is a Red.
If I were Agent and had my wish,
The cad who cheated at shooting fish
    Would get it about the head.
It's not that killing is not my dish
    (Perhaps I would have him hung)
But mechanism is sissyish
Which hedges against the chance the fish
    Will shoot you first instead
        Draw faster and
    Shoot you first instead.

I never shoot fish in an AquaLung
    Whatever the pain or peril.
I never shoot fish in an AquaLung;
    I shoot from the rim of the barrel.
I never shoot fish in an AquaLung,
    Not even the cussedest cods,

Not even the haddock however vicious,
Not even the flounder, and he's delicious,
Not even the shark because Sharks Ain't Fishes —
   It might unbalance the odds
       In fact
   It might unbalance the barrel.

SCENE OF
THE ACCIDENT

The man is dead.
Turn to another.
That holy father
giving the nod —
he should thank God
he can't tell whether
his kind of bother
has profited.

What runts and sports
we do save breed
business and bread
for our cohorts.

Business and bread.
It takes all sorts.

JUST A LITTLE OL' SONG

But what's that under the catalpa blossom
that just went pop and rolled over with a sigh?

Lift up your crinoline, Cindy, hurry on by;
only a possum could play such stinking possum.

God's in his heaven up in the heavy gossamer.
Nothing but blessings tumble out of the sky.

Nothing but wonders well from the sullen bessemer.
Never you scrunch your shoulders, never you cry.

Bad man stammer and fumble when you address him.
Your little foot go swathed in a gauze of Yes'm.

Wolf back away a safe infinitessim,
lolling the laggard lip, the yellow eye.

CAPITAL, JUST CAPITAL

The Law is
   possibly the kindest
      form of death.

The Letter
   killeth, but the Spirit
      deadeneth

to any
   but its own mellifluous
      waste of breath.

80

from Baudelaire: LE GUIGNON

To lift such weight — to start
Lifting — would take the heart
Of Sisyphus: the art
Is long, and time is short.

Far from any tomb
Where a cortège might come,
My heart, like a muffled drum,
Parades — da da dum, da dum.

Many a buried rare
Jewel is sleeping where
No pick or spade intrudes.

Flowers are yielding their
Sweet secrets to the air
Of these deep solitudes.

from Baudelaire:
"Avec ses vêtements"

With her clothes undulating into a thousand colors,
Even when she walks you would think she was dancing,
Or think of those tall serpents the holy jugglers
Weave into ecstasies at the ends of their wands.

Like Algeria, like the flat blue over it,
Like the long swell and counter-swell of the sea,
She lets herself happen with an indifference
Free from disdain or malice: merciless.

Those eyes, the pick of the polished semiprecious;
That strangeness, symbol of anything; that blend
In which only gold, steel, light and diamond enter:
Inviolate angel — sphinx of ages — star —

The very star her hangdog dark companion
Bad-time Charlie the poet names "stérile."

from Baudelaire: LE REBELLE

An angel swoops from his into the fool's
Paradise, snatches up the sinner and
Shakes him, saying, "You're gonna know the rules
Or else. I'm your Good Angel, understand?

Get this: you gotta love (no faces, mind you)
The featherbrained, the half-assed, the off-key,
So Jesus when he comes in state will find you
Spread like a carpet of sweet charity.

That's Love, if you want Love: no pat orgasm
Letting you off the hook: it's pure, it's hot,
It's God's own fire: you burn for all you got!"

Exemplifying his enthusiasm,
He loves the sinner more the more he flays him —
The more, the more he answers, "I cannot!"

TRANSLATIONS FROM
THE ENGLISH

for Arthur Freeman

Pigfoot (with Aces Under) Passes

The heat's on the hooker.
Drop's on the lam.
Cops got Booker.
Who give a damn?

The Kid's been had
But not me yet.
Dad's in his pad.
No sweat.

Margaret Are You Drug

Cool it Mag.
Sure it's a drag
With all that green flaked out.
Next thing you know they'll be changing the color of bread.

But look, Chick,
Why panic?
Sevennyeighty years, we'll *all* be dead.

Roll with it, Kid.
I did.
Give it the old benefit of the doubt.

I mean leaves
Schmeaves.
You sure you aint just feeling sorry for yourself?

Lamb

Lamb, what makes you tick?
You got a wind-up, a Battery-Powered,
A flywheel, a plug-in, or what?
You made out of real Reelfur?
You fall out the window you bust?
You shrink? Turn into a No-No?
Zip open and have pups?

I bet you better than that.
I bet you put out by some other outfit.
I bet you don't do nothin.
I bet you somethin to eat.

Daddy Gander's Newfound Runes

Rain, rain, grow the hay.
Grow the weeds another day.
If I die before I wake,
Skip it.

Little Boy Blue come blow.
   Can't Man; learning a new instrument.
What's with the old one? Where'd you get the new one?
   Found it in a haystack Man.

Old Mother Hubbard,
Decently covered,
Went to her final reward.

She had to laugh.
Manger was half
Empty and half kennel.

Might've known
Old Church been living on
Principal.

I fired a missile up.
It came down maybe.
Maybe it stayed up.
Things aint much like they used to be.

84

BALLADE OF
THE MISLAID WORKSHEET

for Bernard Weinberg

Where are the notes I made last year
On the flip side of a popcorn package
Toward my perennial sacrilege
Upon the Muse: another near-
Translation of Villon? But where
Is Harlow? Where is Norma Tallmadge?
Norma Jean Baker? Norma Shearer?
What tantalizing curve or cleavage — ?
   Water under the bridge.

Back to my dog-eared Dictionnaire.
Back to my Fowler's *English Usage*.
But where is Mrs. Average
American? Remember her —
Smiling at her discoverer
The census-man — a Personage
At last? And Carole Lombard, where
Is she? And Mrs. Calvin Coolidge?
   Water under the bridge.

Where are the powers I bargain for:
The Archimedean leverage
To raise at least my own dead language
Up? O Edmund Spenser, where
In the wildern woods of verbiage
Hath wonèd wended, and whither yore?
And oomph, and eld, and yesteryear?
And Bernhardt's voice, and Bernhardt's carriage?
   Water under the bridge.

L'envoi

A thousand scattered cans of footage
Turning in unison yellower,
A piece of French Literature,
And this, a petty pilferage
On both, are yours awhile, and are
    Water under the bridge.

BALLADE FOR
RATTLE AND BRUSHES

May Day for sure: new monarchs nod
    above their stricken fetters;
the grassroots fire their fusillade
    of bright attention-getters;
and who's to care or think it odd
if each insurgent gang has trod
under a grizzled awkward-squad
    of aiders and abetters
    as homely as old sweaters?
Who's to complain? What utter clod?

Busying every floweret
    with touselers and prodders,
molesting mint and mignonette
    with aerial hot-rodders,
loaded and looped as it can get,
dizzier than the violet
whose petals arch like a quintet
    of whirling eisteddfodders,
    May is. The gray vine dodders
and gets more looped, more loaded yet.

Green legions rise through a glissade
    of keepers and begetters —
of husk and chrysalis and pod

86

deferring to their betters,
and who's to care or think it odd?
If sod-banked fires of goldenrod
leap to obliterate the sod,
    should they fold up like debtors?
    explain themselves in letters?
Who says as much? What utter clod?

L'envoi

Far be it, my Scheherezade,
from oaten straw or dried peascod
    to be the oversetters
of any ordinance of God
so just, so gay, so iron-shod.
One may be dead as the ballade
but not, as yet, an utter clod.

BALLADE OF
THE GOLDEN RULE

To Lord Russell

When the fat priest looks up from his oolong
and tells me that Mercy shineth in God's sight
in the voice of a three-year-old coached in a popular song,
he tells me right, although he has no right.
And when Carolyi, his fingers in permanent flight
and his words unable to get back where they belong,
tells me the simple truth it cost him sight,
sons, daughters to learn, he tells me wrong.

When the well-heeled escapee from Hong Kong
graces his talk on the Menace of Communist Might
with the thought that Only Our Love Shall Make Us Strong,
he tells me right, although he has no right.
And when Big Henry, back at his broom in spite
of the Ford ignition coil and the jackboot thong,
gives me an unimpassioned black-and-white
of the old As Is as it is, he tells me wrong.

There is no justice. The lump with the Huey Long
galluses and the diffidence of a Birchite,
beating the Book like his own personal gong,
can tell me right, though he has no more right
to gospel at me than to sleep at night
while the night does business elsewhere hammer and tong.
But *teach* the boy, show him the appetite
of the air for his own screams, he'll tell me wrong.

L'envoi

Bertie, you mathematical blatherskite,
you knew all this. You held fast for so long.
You seemed so uninstructible in the right
of wrongs to exact their modicum of wrong.

IV

WARPAINT

POEMS FROM THE 1970s,
FROM THE BOOK **DESPERATE MEASURES**

THE SAD BALLAD
OF THE FIFTEEN CONSECUTIVE RHYMES

The woods exuded woodsiness;
  The meadows lay inviting;
Amantha Roin rose to address
Her Summer Worshop in Creative Writing —
  Amantha Roin the poetess,
    Close-barbered and exciting.

Amantha was a Formalist
  And yet her voice grew mellow
As through a Late Romantic mist
  Of mauve and taupe and yellow
She glimpsed the Koh-i-noor of her class list:
  The Fellowfeeling Fellow.

The Fellowfeeling Fellowship
  Of Middleburger College
Had fallen (with tuition, board, and haulage)
  Upon the Sheik of Serendip.
  Amantha Roin stood in the grip
Of feelings she could only half acknowledge:

A loaf of rye, a jug of rye,
  A bough of Bo or Banyan:
Her muse had skipped off on the sly
  To Wimpole Street, or Stanyan.
Her eyes were stars, each starry eye
Occulted by a sultry dark companion.

And dark, dark as his gaze remained,
  Darker were his intentions,
And dark his English usage, strained
  Through Arabic declensions,
And dark the crude oil that maintained
A retinue of staggering dimensions.

But how, by all that gushes forth,
  By all that blackly glisters,
Had such a catch been angled North
  Beyond the Seven Sisters,

Beyond fair Haverford, and Swarth-
More redolent with luscious war-resisters?

Was he some petro-prospector
    Or Black November hit man
Biding his time like Aaron Burr,
    Disguised as a Comp-Lit man
    And idiot idolater
Of Ed Dorn and the late great Walter Whitman?

In days when workshops clanked aloud
    And turned an honest dollar,
A Benefactor had endowed
In what was then a frugal proud
    School for the turned of collar
A fellowship for some poor foreign scholar.

He was to be of Heathen Race
    But Protestant Vocation,
And those benighted tribes whom Grace
Had allocated tenting-space
    On Biblical location
Were to be given First Consideration.

In course of time Endowments grow
    But seminarists scarcen.
They sought among the Esquimaux,
    The Ainu, the Arapaho,
The Jain, the Cree, and (constantly) the Saracen.
The dearth of True Vocations was embarrassing.

(I've left Amantha poised to speak.
    Oh do not think me caddish.
Would I could let her spend the week
    There, blushing like a radish —
Amantha Roin, of all her clique
    Most distant and most faddish.)

The College was endowed as much
    With moxie as with money.
Its Deans convened a local clutch
Of Etymologists and such
Who solved the problem so fast it was funny.
I give you their solution: it's a honey:

"If we ask what exactly are
    The *roots* of this dilemma,"
One said, "we need not question far:
For 'Seminarist,' *Seminar*.
    Unless I misremember,
    We held one last September."

"We did, we did," his colleagues said,
    "The Writers' Workshop held it!"
And thus, in time, there vibrated,
    So that it almost felled it,
Within Amantha's trunk her red
    Red heart. Could she have spelled it,

She would have doodled "Thine" in Arabic
Across her lecture notes. It made her sick
That she whose very dreams came out in couplets
Now seemed *enceinte* with butterfly quintuplets
Whilst he, if he looked ill and rolled his eyes,
Groaned not for her, but for her Exercise.

And true enough, Amantha gave
    The Devil's own Assignments,
Like making amphybrachs behave
    In trimeter alignments
With triple rhyme and other grave
    And devious refinements.

And true as well, her paladin,
Whose chill taskmistress she had been
    For fear of being other,
Had borne things from his "Miss Ro-in"
    He wouldn't from his mother.
Last Friday she had given him another:

"Exercise 9. A narrative
    In stanza form containing
At least fifteen consecutive
    Rhymes." He was past complaining.
A dying *bulbul,* he would give
    What strength he had remaining.

93

For seven days and seven nights
   He neither slept nor laundered.
Perhaps he brooded on his rights.
   Perhaps his reason wandered.
Perhaps he tasted the delights
   Of hashish as he pondered.

In any case, as all the great
   Wire services reported,
He swept his burnoose from a pate
   That glistened and contorted,
Took sudden stance before the late
   Amantha Roin, and snorted

Unintelligible gutturals.
Imagine the mad race of Miss Roin's pulse —
His eyes, her notes, the students, his brown fist,
His eyes, his dangling glasses, and now this
Dazzling damascus blade cleaving the air —
By all that's Formal, let us leave her there.

   Time shall not tarnish, Gentlemen,
  That classic of composure when
     She steadied herself and knew
     She would either be chopped in two
     Or chopped into a whole lot,
     Depending of course on what
        fur-
        ther,
           per-
           ver-
           ser
                mur-
                der-
                er
   her
           Ber-
           ber
                Ber-
                ser-
                ker
                    were.

THE VISIT

The gingerbread house in the gingerbread forest,
  That's where it took place.
The gin, the St. Vitus, the gingivitis,
  Whatever it was, her face

Was radiant. The kids were zonked.
  Even the mice were de-
Molished on an overdose
  Of stone patisserie.

Grandmama in her thermal formal,
  Grandpapa in his cape,
Had just settled down for a paranormal
  Nightcap at the nape

When out in the clutter of Forest Lawn
  Stone furniture there landed
A wee little ship, from whose wee little hatch
  There strode forth, openhanded,

A wee little man with his little ol' eyes
  So shifty and lightning-quick
That we knew right away — oh *what* a surprise —
  That it must be TrickyDick.

He was chuckling all over and licking and grinning and
  Ooh, this was getting fun!
He was checking the house for chimneys. Nope.
  And for doors. There was just the one. . . .

Oh goodie he found it. Around he bounded,
  Casing the joint for green.
Casing the joint for red. Confounded
  Snooper he was, and mean.

He knew what a stocking was used for: to hang!
  And goodies for kiddies: to hide!

To hide from the sniveling beggars! We sprang
   For the door. In the nick! Outside!

We twisted the key in the gingerbread lock
   In the patented blast-proof door,
And that's why no one's terrified
   At Christmas anymore.

But Christmas Eve, or Halloween,
   Or *any* susceptible season,
I wouldn't go down to the gingerbread wood
   If I didn't have terrible reason.

I think I would rather sit down on a *thistle*
   Than listen to that. And to hear him excite
A yet clammier gaggle of slimier creatures
   To wail and to wallow? Good night.

ERRAND

Buckety-buckety,
Susan B. Anthony
Strode to the bench to be
Charged by the Judge:

"Hyperaesthenia!
Flibbertigibbetry!
Hogwash! Hysterical
Feminist fudge!"

CHIP

Clippety cloppety,
Cesare Borgia
Modeled himself on his
Father the Pope:

Pontifex Maximus,
Paterfamilias,
Generalissimo:
Able to cope.

SAID

Agatha Christie to
E. Phillips Oppenheim,
"Who is this Hemingway,
Who is this Proust?

Who is this Vladimir
Whatchamacallum, this
Neopostrealist
Rabble?" she groused.

SAID

J. Alfred Prufrock to
Hugh Selwyn Mauberly,
"What ever happened to
Senlin, ought-nine?"

"One with the passion for
Orientalia?"
"Rather." "Lost track of him."
"Pity." "Design."

SAID

Dame Edith Evans to
Margaret Rutherford,
"Seance? Oh really, my
Dear, if there be

Nonhypothetical
Extraterrestrial
Parapsychologists,
They can call *me*."

SIBERIA

Albany schmalbany.
Governor W.
Averell Harriman
Hated the place.

Bunch of Albanians.
Think he was some kind of
Megalopolitan
Charity case.

HIGH RENAISSANCE

"Nomine Domini
Theotocopoulos,
None of these prelates can
Manage your name.

Change it. Appeal to their
Hellenophilia.
Sign it 'El Greco.' I'll
Slap on a frame."

MONARCH OF THE SEA

"Jiminy Whillikers,
Admiral Samuel
Eliot Morison,
Where is your ship?"

"I, sir, am HMS
Historiography's
Disciplinarian.
Button your lip."

VOYAGE OF DISCOVERY

Higgledy piggledy,
Governor-General-
Designate James Edward
Oglethorpe wept.

Three more incipient
Okeefenokian
Octogenarians
Born as he slept.

TWIGS

for Lore Segal

Ludwig van Beethoven
Slept often and ate often,
Combed seldom and cared less,
Causing his friends considerable distress.

Baron von Richthofen
Urped often and hicked often.
His friends knew what to do.
They would sneak up behind him and go Boo.

Michelangelo
Could not be his Mummsy's daddy, so
He had to become Italy's
Praxiteles.

BOSTON

Mr. Paul Verlaine?
We've come to fix your clerihew again.
No no no no, moi je m'appelle Verlaine.
Sure buddy, and I'm Richard Henry Dana.

STOCKHOLM

Rabindranath Tagore
Made flowers bloom where there were none before.
"It's my green thumb," he said, "and with my tan
    thumb
I do stuff like the Indian National Anthem."

ALEXANDER THE GREAT, PART I

Higgledy piggledy,
Philip of Macedon
Gave his young son an un-
Breakable horse.

Lacedemonian
Pusillanimity
Followed therefrom as a
Matter of course.

ALEXANDER THE GREAT, PART II

Higgledy piggledy,
Pindar the Scrivener
Stared from the one erect
Doorway in Thebes.

Exquisite study in
Vulnerability.
Offered as such to the
Spartan ephebes.

ALEXANDER THE GREAT, PART III

Higgledy piggledy,
Emperor Darius
Found his dependencies
Gaza and Tyre

Put to a radical
Gastrointestinal
Physiotherapy,
Then to the fire.

ALEXANDER THE GREAT, PART IV

Higgledy piggledy,
Bucephalopolis
Falls to the Indians,
Tyre to the Medes.

Homogeneity?
Manageability?
Aristotelean
Wind in the reeds.

ALEXANDER THE GREAT, PART V

Higgledy piggledy
David Ben Gurion,
Higgledy piggledy
Shah of Iran.

Saudi Arabian
Geomorphology
Launches a thousand-foot
Ship in Japan.

FALLING ASLEEP OVER SCOTT

for Anthony Hecht

Drowsing one day in The
Heart of Midlothian,
Finding no pillow to
Cushion my head,

Reaching for Kenilworth,
Happening onto an
Earlier Waverly
Novel instead,

Why was I suddenly
Bound, on the battlements,
Helpless to rescue my
Self from the dread

Castle of Torquilstone's
Phantasmagoria,
While a bull voice from the
Parapet said

"Runagate ruffian,
Wilfred of Ivanhoe,
Whom dost thou sally at?
Whom dost thou seek?

Brian de Bois-Guilbert?
Reginald Front-de-Boeuf?
Lucas de Beaumanoir?
Rabbi Ben Samuel?

Stephen de Martival?
William de Mareschal?
Oldhelm of Malmsbury?
Jacob Ben Tudela?
Richard Plantagenet,

Alias Lion-Heart,
Latterly Knight of the
Fetterlock? Eke

Herman of Goodalricke?
Cedric of Rotherwood?
Dennis the Cellarer?
Giles de Mauleverer?
Richard de Malvoisin?
Philip de Malvoisin?
Albert de Malvoisin,
Master of Templestowe?
Locksley of Nottingham,
Formerly Huntingdon,
Alias Robin Hood?
Gaultier of Middleton?
Ulfgar of Middleham?
Hilda of Middleham?
Athelstane Adelingson,
Franklin of Coningsburgh?
Whom wouldst thou duel or
Diplodactylify?
Scarify? Vilify?
Pole-axe or pique?

Call the man out! Be he
Anglonormanophobe
Churl from our charnel or
Cock of our clique,

Spit him you shall! give his
Skippety-hoppity
Madrigal-monicker
Back in his cheek!

Skewer them, scatter them,
Hyperpersnickety
Gaggle of gluttonous
Gabblemouth geeks!

'Top o' the morning, Miss
Ulrica Wolfganger.'
'Thankee, good Nathan Ben
Israel.' — Breeks'

104

Bones! The bare minimum
Breakfast amenities
Drive a man mad in a
Matter of weeks!

Who in the name of the
Quasihistorical
Sent me this houseful of
Metrical freaks?"

Long rang the echoes from
Breastworks to bulwark to
Outwork to catwalk through
Dungeon and hall.

Longer still, silence, till
TrumanCapotean
Vocables rose from the
Base of the wall:

"Crotchety-crotchety,
Fictional Spokesperson:
Dactylophobiac
Tantrums like these

Scarcely bespeak the com-
Posure demanded of
One who would wrestle a
Folk to its knees.

As for my *challenge,* you
Blankety-blankety
Bounder, convey my re-
Spects to that Non-

U, that non-ullulant
Monosyllabical
Name of a name, the u-
Surper *King John!*"

Noises of battle rolled
In and rolled over me.
Cauldrons of pitch were up-
Ended in flame.

105

Stones were hurled earthward, then
Garbage, then carcasses,
Timbers, bound prisoners,
Me!   Was my name

Saved from the wreck of that
Keep in some chronicle?
Saved for some reader years
Hence? As for me,

I like to think it a
Nonprobability
Epiphenomeno-
Logically.

I like to think that the
Waverly Novelist
Nodded and wavered and
Vanished in smoke

Like a closed book, like a
Saudi Arabian
Djinn, like a higgledy
Pig in a poke.

DESPERATE MEASURES

Oh Momma, Momma, I haven't slept for weeks.
This secretary and I are being blackmailed by a bunch of sheiks.
I thank my stars it's Henry they've been to see.
I don't know how I could stand it if they came straight to me
With their oily insinuations and their bedroom millinery

Henry, Momma. What do you mean "What Henry?"
Henry the *Secretary* I've been talking about
That the Sheiks are after because of the way that we've all made out
And now we gotta get money so we can pay them and keep them quiet
And he's a lovely warm human person and a real laff riot
But what if silence is like happiness and you can buy it
And buy it and buy it and it just won't stay bought?
Bad enough with the pot fiends rioting in the streets.
But blackmail! *Trading* on another person's dirty secrets.
It's worse than being a classified-documents-leaker, it's
Diabolicaller it's slimier it's sneakier it's

Blackmail! Oh Momma I just don't care anymore.
They can drag our impetuous ardor in all its sordor
Into the glare of the lawcourts and the even horrider
Glint in the eye of the would-be boudoir toreador
The *Suck-of-the-Month* subscriber the *PlayboyPortfolio*reader
The plain-brown-wrapper *Scenes-from-the-Life-of-Ann-Corio*orderer —

Blackmail! Plastered in tabloid all over the porno shops.

I shall stand there shattered, defenseless, hopeless, topless
And throw myself on the generosity of the American populace.
It worked all right for the Pinochets and the PapaDocs and the
     Papadopouloses.
It works for the nattering-kneejerk internationalist applepolishers
And their eastern establishment limousine lib-lab scuttlebuttpublishers,
And if I can just get a little groundswell started among the Winnetkans and
     the Tuhungans, Gee:

I can hear me now: *Gent*lepersons of the Petit Jury,
What's the big rap here? Mayhem? Kickbacks? Jobbery?
Some scheme of evil rivaling in its obduracy

The Crédit Mobilier and the Teapot Dome?
Why *hang* it all, we just puttin' a little down-home
Jalapeno chilipepper into the implementation of
Nation-to-nation nonstop marathon stratamatic love-sweet-love.

World I could love you to death.
The Kid from Nazareth
Said that. And the World best listen. Hell to pay.
Love you to death, said Dennis and Doris Day.
And Martha and Johnny and Sanjit and James Earl Ray.

World I could love you to death
The great Hernan Cortez
Sang as he jangled down to Tenochtitlan,
And Sammy and Idris and Herman and Genghis Khan
And the Madames Lafarge, Chiang, Bovary, Cho-Cho-San
Jostle along. And Alvin Dark. And Jeanne.
It's the universal background *music,* Mon.

World I could love you to death.
Give in to it. So saith
Good old Elizabeth
I, II, Berrigan, Bagaya, Borden-and-I-don't-mean-cow.
You better believe it, Wayne Babe. Dr. Lao
Said it, Mao
Said it, the entire cast of the festival at Oberammergau
Said it and durned if there isn't this kind of a massed ancestral row
That builds up into my bloodstream like a thunderhead over the Jungfrau
Or a tidal wave or a Ghost with a notion to say it and say it now:

Evvvvvrybody go kidnap Henry Kissinger.
Evvvvvrybody go kid —
                         Aw come on. Oh wow,
You must have had goofy-juice with your evening chow.
That went out with Spock. With the Rome Plow.
Might as well tell me huelga. Tell me Dow.
Might as well tell me giftshop Handy Wrappinger. How?

Just everybody go kidnap Henry Kissinger.
Fill skin of head with sand.
Place out in sun.

Just everybody go kidnap Henry Kissinger.
fill skin of head with ashdust.
Place by stream.

Just everybody go kissify Henry Kidnap.

108

Fill skin of head with cool.
Place in high place.

Whaddaya trine? Whaddaya make me? Play the fool?
I got no time. Gotta nab me a bullshit heiress.
Nab me a Yanqui plantboss.
Nab some yids.
Kidnap the didn'ts. Kidnap the diddly dids.

Whoa there, Cha-Cha, line up and place your bids.
Them penny-ante contracts is for kids.
Goddamit, this is *crime.*
Have I been getting through to you? This time
It's everybody kidnap everybody.
Hold for extravagant ransom.
Keep secure.

It's everybody in bad hands. Everybody
Off to fantabulous hideouts.
Gone to earth.

That's everybody. You got that? Everybody.
No bystanders. No stragglers.
No fifth wheels.

Now everybody *glare* at everybody.
Listen, you're my investment.
You get sick,

Then *everybody* loses. Everybody
Finish his goddam oatmeal.
Nice and thick.

Now everybody snarl. Give everybody
Beautiful hardboiled reasons.
Companions. Eggs.

Now everybody count off. Everybody?
Single exception, Captain.
Heavens! Who?

Henry? Out there alone with Man-with-
Suitcase? Ooh.

Nobody out there now but Man-with-Suitcase.
Black Samsonite suitcase.
All that loot.

Practicing to himself: "Put down that suitcase!"
Practicing to himself: "Stop or I'll shoot!"

DEDICATION

To my mother the rewrite expert,
who took impossible books and set them straight,
whose blue pencil and whose gray IBM electric typewriter
    made such a steady business in the little apartment,
who could reach to the heart with two fists, fixing the gibberish-monster
    patiently, firmly, politely by the throat
    until the whole fierce fluttering armory of theatrics
    reared up and collapsed like a house of crockery,
who knew from repeated experience the weird likelihood
    that here, too, under the commencement warpaint,
    cowered the watchful intelligence of some stripling
    kidnapped into the tribe of the Ed Professors,
who had seen it all in the study of her father the silver-maned prairie
        educator
    and in the studio of her mother the mother-of-seven and concert pianist,
who had learned a few things too as a wartime Wilshire bus driver,
and who made a precarious living applying wisdom without credential
    in Godforsaken Los Angeles,
dedication
    is just the sort of word
    you would expect to find floating around
    in the hot air looking for a place to settle:
Dedication to this and that high purpose.
Dedication to deep ancestral values.
Dedication to
    and you could hear her laughing.

WORKING HABITS

Federico García Lorca
used to uncork a
bottle or two of wine
whenever the duende dwindled for a line.

James Joyce
would have preferred a choice
of brandies in decanters made by Tiffany's,
but rotgut was the shortcut to epiphanies.

The Later Henry James
bet shots of rum against himself in games
of how much can we pyramid upon a
given donné.

Little Dylan Thomas
didn't keep his promise
to stay out of Milk Wood.
He tried to drown the fact as best he could.

Anna Akhmatova
Eyed the last shot of a
Pre-war *cognac de champagne.*
"So much for you, little brandy. *Do svidanya.*"

T. S. Eliot
used to belly it
up to the nearest bar,
then make for a correlative objective in his car.

Proust
used
to
too.

SONNET WITH A DIFFERENT LETTER
AT THE END OF EVERY LINE

for Helen Vendler

O for a muse of fire, a sack of dough,
Or both! O promissory notes of woe!
One time in Santa Fe N.M.
Ol' Winfield Townley Scott and I . . . But whoa.

One can exert oneself, *ff,*
Or architect a heaven like Rimbaud,
Or if that seems, how shall I say, *de trop,*
One can at least write sonnets, a propos
Of nothing save the do-re-mi-fa-sol
Of poetry itself. Is not the row
Of perfect rhymes, the terminal bon mot,
Obeisance enough to the Great O?

"Observe," said Chairman Mao to Premier Chou,
"On voyage à Parnasse pour prendre les eaux.
On voyage comme poisson, incog."

TUOLOMNE

(Tu·ol'·omn·e. 1. a river in California, north of
the Yosemite. 2. a meadowland on the river,
above Hetch-Hetchy. 3. a tribe, now vanished.)

for Meg Nye

Lord, look at the grass.
Globs, glebes, gallopings, a whole ocean
and blade after blade after blade
of promiscuous
grass.
It could make a man feel called.
Called on the carpet.
Yes, Lord, yes,
I let my seed fall on the rocky ground.
I never laid my talents out to found
The many-mansioned condominium.
I stop off to camp out on the way home
From a trip west to see my married daughter
And look at me.
                    Big woodsman.
                                    I'm so dumb
I build my nylon dreamhouse on the sand.

You read me well enough.
Mornings, chilled to the marrow, when I stand
And squint out over the pebble-brightening water,
Something there is that shakes me by the scruff.

I forage off. I climb a little bluff
And kick my morning cat-hole in the dirt.
My knees are cold. They hurt.
I get down close to what my heel turned over.
All made of leaves! Oh look:
So many profligacies brought to book.
Look at the way the crumbs and fragments glisten.

Tell me again thy teachings, Lord, I'll listen.

Happy the man who hunkers down and mulls
A second reading of the parables.
It hungers up the blood and whets the air.
The *things* that are entrusted to my care!

Where there is soil, plant seed. Where there is boulder,
Cover the same with buildings. Neither build
Nor scatter seed along the highway shoulder,
But if you are an ethnic, scavenge there
For someone newly robbed, or damn near killed,
Or both, whom it behooves you to befriend.
If you are merely indigent, perpend:
The hedges and the ditches are the place
To stand forth and be feculent in case
Some parvenu who planned a banquet gets
A mailboxful of monogrammed regrets
And throws himself a little social tantrum.
If someone slips you money, don't succumb
To modesty or misplaced moral scruple.
Throw it around! Invest! It might quadruple.
Weeds, you weed out. Collect the weed seed, though.
Your enemy may sink *his* pot of gold
In millet-fields and leave them unpatrolled.
Salt, you are meant to savor, not to sow,
Unless there is a grievance to avenge.
On sand, thou shalt not build nor plant nor scavenge,
But meditate. The sand shall be a standard
Of competition and comparison
In counting up the offspring of the dutiful.
The lily too shall function. It is beautiful.
Lastly, at unpredicted interval,
A sparrow shall conveniently fall
To test the quickness of the Cosmic Eyeball.

I have committed whimsy. There. So be it.
I have not followed wisdom as I see it.
You avalanche me sermons and I make
Rhymes for the sake of rhymes.
Break
This tippy-toe transgressor of his crimes.

It's not as if you hadn't, lots of times,
Shown me the moon.
The kingdom brought to birth.
Convulsion in the ferns. The very earth
Rising above itself in ecstasies.
Haven't I gone glass-eyed onto my knees
To pry into the busyness of these
Green legions, every microscopic blob
A roller-palace with a milling mob
Of chloroplasts careening around in it
A dozen or two dozen times a minute?
How furious they are as they compete
At drawing water up a hundred feet
To let a picturebook blue spruce complete
Its simulacrum of a waterfall.
A man'd have to think exceeding small
To get no hustle from that plasmic jazz.
Quadrillions! Every cell as frenzied as
A Circus Maximus beside a Tiber.
Whole generations toughen into fiber
And turn into the body of the mother
While I scratch out one verbal razzmatazz
And heavy up my notebook with another.
They have their conquests to consolidate.
And I?
I guess I'm here to celebrate
Myself, your works, man's passions, or the State,
Depending on which school I emulate.

And do I mock?
I mock.
And grieve?
I grieve.
There's nothing I would gladlier achieve
Than Poetry. I mean the serious thing.
Not this Pop-Popean ring-a-ding-dinging.

The pure Organic Form,

Where not one word malingers from the norm
Of grateful dedication to a purpose
Higher than its own accidental likings.
As self-effacing as a bunch of Sherpas,

As drab as doughboys and as dour as Vikings,
Ready to take the universe by storm
And die in the attempt, my Words would swarm
Over the dazzled reader like a . . . swarm.
Of bees perhaps. Or how are wasps at swarming?
O hell, the whole conception was just *forming*.
I *know* that poem. I can almost *hear* it,
So sure am I of it, and of the spirit
In which I have heard (so often) it described.

I'd swear I struck the rock once and imbibed
Something that wasn't used-up hock-and-soda.
Move like the wind upon these waters, Lord;
Make me a spectacle of devastations;
Break, blow, batter me, leave me floored
And at the mercy of the Great Inflation
That launched Jack Keats. Or was it Carol Doda?

Hopeless, abysmal, my transgression is.
You are, by your own double-barreled Testament,
An agribusiness tipster and a whiz
At principles of capital investment,
And here, instead of pyramiding shares,
I'm scattering my corn among the tares,
As bad as any of those silly gooses
Who put the right thing to the wrong thing's uses
And made an utter hash of their affairs.

I'd better just sit down.
I'd better get my coffee boiled, and brown
An egg or two around the spitting edges,
And sop them with that canned brown bread I love.
I'd better take a walk into the scenery
And on the willows in the midst thereof
Philosophize without so much machinery.

Great big lumberless weeds,
What are you good for? Holding sand together?
Huddling in bunches under heavy weather
Like immigrants on shipboard? That would fit.
The cabin-class contingent lathers it
Off to the high horizon hell-for-leather
And there you stay, all sombre on the decks
Of something big and frightening and just

About to give in to an underthrust
And go down in the folklore of great wrecks.

I've seen you walk the waters, willow trees.
Somewhere in all their dappled botanies
I think the English Bards ran out of gas.
They left you lorn, and pretty much unheeded,
Except when one of their fair damsels needed
A semiotic shorthand for Alas.

No skin off you. Who needs us and our tricks,
Our amateur hysterics and theatrics?

I've seen you skating with an easy stroke
On waters that would petrify an oak.
I've seen you lean, and brake, and send a slash
Of icy whiteness up against a trash
Of aspen-bones and ponderosa rubble
The snow-melt-water flood had swept aside
Like scaffolding. I've seen your streamers ride
The wind as if to whip it on the double
And laugh at it for getting out of breath.
I've seen you scare a camper half to death
You stood so calm, so silent and serene.
He thought he almost knew what it would mean
To cease upon the midnight without cavil.
He tossed his beans aside, and panned some gravel,
And whistled "Oh My Darling Clementine"
To put his thoughts back into proper channels.
And when he'd pulled up stakes, and itched his flannels,
He *still* felt shivers up and down his spine.

Some master of the high Miltonic line
Owes you a Great Ode, willows, sure as hell.
I think I'll speak about it to Kinnell.
I hate to see so versatile a tree gypped
Out of its rightful place in the Anthology.

But this is not some Ode, it's an Apology.
And if it needs a moral, there's the grass.

Look at it. Grass grass grass.
Who sent these indolent armies out of Egypt?
They pillow the plains and valleys wall-to-wall.

I do, Lord, oh I do wait for a call.
But also, I enjoy my avocations.
I scribble side-notes to the fall of nations.
I play with spacings, and with indentations.
And generally, I sit here like a dope,
As obviated as the spheres of Ptolemy,
And keep my crafts and hobbies up, and hope
That when the big wind comes, it speaks Tuolomne.

I mean why not? I know the wind I seek
To flee from seven days an average week.
If everything it says to me is Greek,
And everything it means to me is All,
And all I care about is the unknown,
Who is to say I'm loco if I fall
Into a little singsong of my own,
And while the twigs fly, and the tent-ropes moan,
I make a joyful noise: "You speak Tuol-
Omne. You speak Tuolomne. You speak
Tuolomne."

ACKNOWLEDGMENTS

1: Thin Ice

Agni Review: Sunday Brunch in the Boston Restoration
The Atlantic: The Spell Against Spelling; The Staunch Maid and the
 Extraterrestrial Trekkie
Carolina Quarterly: The Great Dam Disaster a Ballad
Chicago Review: Magnificat in Transit from the Toledo Airport (in part,
 under the title Ode in a Time of Industrial Diversification)
Iowa Review: Canon Fanin's Apology
Ploughshares: The Sixth Fleet Still out There in the Mediterranean, under
 the title Mykonos, Wall with Mailbox
Poetry: On Gozzoli's Painted Room in the Medici Palace; The Universe Is
 Closed and Has REMs; Sonnet in the Shape of a Potted Christmas Tree
Pomegranate: Sign

4: Warpaint

The poem The Visit is not included in *Desperate Measures*; it originally
 appeared in *The New York Review of Books*.